P9-CLS-312

The Cichlid

Howell Book House

Howell Book House
Hungry Minds, Inc.
909 Third Avenue
New York, NY 10022
www.hungryminds.com

For general information on Hungry Minds books in the U.S., please call our Consumer Customer Service department at 800-762-2974. In Canada, please call (800) 667-1115. For reseller information, including discounts and premium sales, please call our Reseller Customer Service department at 800-434-3422.

Library of Congress Cataloging-in-Publication Data
Sweeney, Mary Ellen
The cichlid: an owner's guide to a happy, healthy fish/[Mary E. Sweeney].
p. cm.
Includes bibliographical references
ISBN 1-58245-016-1
1. Cichlids. I. Title.
SF458.C5S93 1999
639.3'774—dc21 98-33422
CIP

Manufactured in the United States of America
10 9 8 7 6 5 4 3

Series Director: Amanda Pisani
Book Design: Michele Laseau
Cover Design: Iris Jeromnimon
Illustration: Steve Adams
Photography: Aaron Norman
Production Team: Carrie Allen, Trudy Coler, Ellen Considine, Kristi Hart, and Heather Pope

Contents

part one

Welcome to the World of the Cichlid

part two

Cichlids in the Home

part three

Kinds of Cichlids

part four

Beyond the Basics

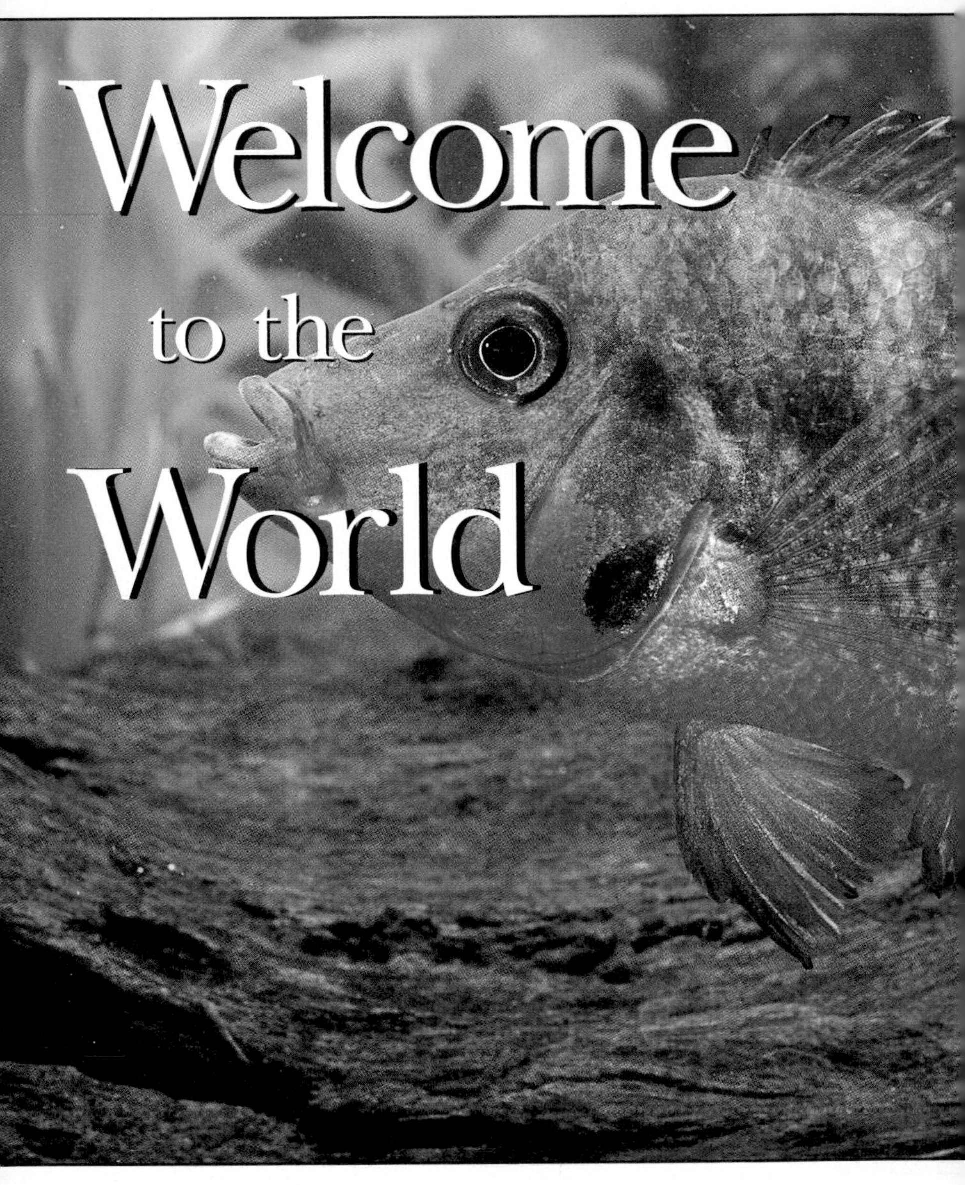
Welcome
to the
World

part one 

of the Cichlid

External Features of the Cichlid

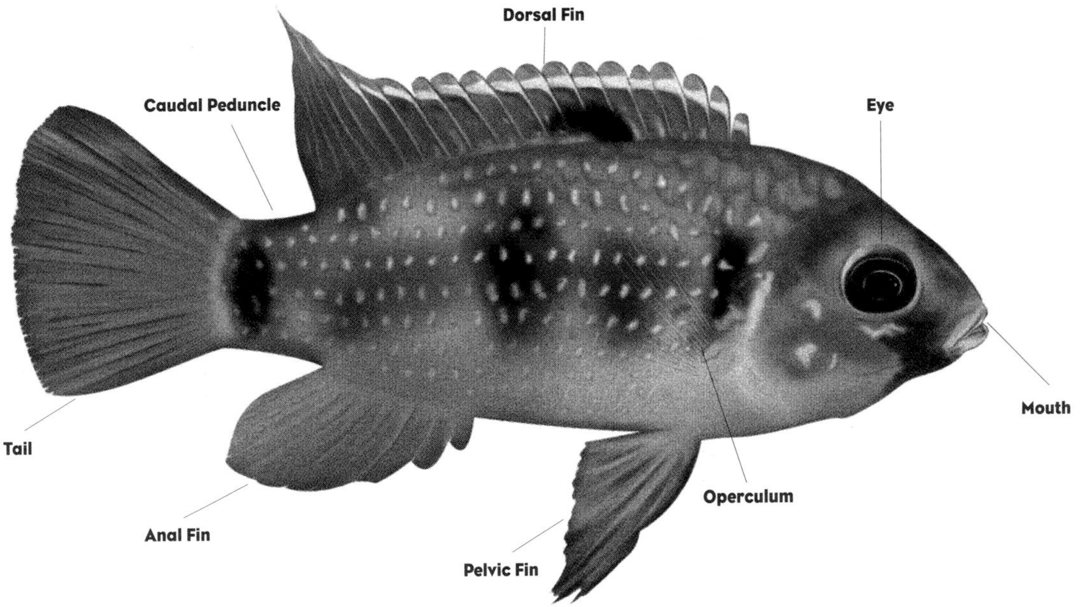

Dorsal Fin

Caudal Peduncle

Eye

Mouth

Tail

Operculum

Anal Fin

Pelvic Fin

chapter 1

What Is a Cichlid?

The family *Cichlidae* contains more than 1,200 species, and these fishes are called cichlids (pronounced *sick*-lids). The majority of the cichlid species are found in tropical Africa, and about 200 species are in Central and South America. One genus, *Etroplus*, is found in parts of Asia.

Cichlids are highly evolved freshwater fishes with origins in marine fishes such as damselfish, wrasses and surfperch. These ancient links with the sea permit them to live in a wide variety of water conditions, including salt content and water hardness. Cichlids can live in waters ranging from extremely hard and alkaline, as do the African rift lake

cichlids, to soft and acidic, as in the case of the South American discus, angelfish and others.

Cichlids originated from marine fishes such as the Damselfish (Neoglyphidodon oxyodon).

Fishkeepers Love Cichlids

Cichlids are the most popular of all the aquarium fishes, partly because there are so many species to choose from. But when you also factor in their vivacious personalities, interesting behavior and considerable good looks, it's no mystery why people are so fascinated with cichlids.

Keeping these ever-popular cichlids is not without some challenges, however. Many have horrible reputations for aggression, predation and general destructiveness. Once you understand the nature of your cichlid, though, you can make accommodations for its behavior. Much of the aggression exhibited by these fish is related to their extraordinary spawning and parental behaviors, and the sight of a pair of cichlids in breeding color leading a large, healthy spawn makes any special attention required well worth the effort.

Cichlid Characteristics

What exactly is a cichlid? It's often impossible to determine from appearance alone whether a fish is a cichlid. Many fishes that look like they could be cichlids actually belong to other unrelated families. The North American sunfishes, *Lepomis* spp., for example, are shaped like some cichlids and have a cichlid "look" but actually are members of the family *Centrarchidae.*

Cichlids are placed in the family *Cichlidae* by ichthyologists—scientists who study fishes—because of their evolutionary history. In appearance, cichlids are small- to medium-sized fish, although they're among the largest fishes kept in aquariums. Their bodies are generally perch-like, but some cichlids, such as the angelfish, are anything but perch-like. Some features are universal among all cichlids: (1) pharyngeal jaws that assist in processing food; (2) one pair of nostrils; (3) a single dorsal fin with hard fin rays in the front; and (4) at least three hard rays in the anal fin. Most cichlids also have a two-part lateral line, which is a row of small holes that runs from behind the eye back along the body of the fish.

COMMON CICHLID TRAITS

The cichlid family is large, and it is difficult to identify a member of the family based solely on appearance. Nonetheless, all cichlids have a few physical attributes in common: pharyngeal jaws for processing food, one pair of nostrils, a single dorsal fin with hard fin rays in the front and a minimum of three hard rays in the anal fin.

Caring for the Young

Cichlids are renowned for the care of their young. All cichlids are egglayers, and most lay their eggs on some sort of surface as opposed to scattering them in the water and then abandoning them, as do so many of the egglayers.

There are many breeding styles among cichlids, but parental care is a major feature of their behavior. Whether the particular species lays its eggs in a cave or on a plant leaf, all cichlids remain with the eggs, guard them until they hatch and then care for the young until they are able to fend for themselves (up to a point!). It is actually this extraordinary parental care that causes so much mayhem in the cichlid aquarium.

Most cichlids have an elongated body; angelfish are an exception to this rule.

Cichlids are very aggressive in defense of their breeding territories, eggs and fry, and there isn't much that can be done about this except to remove all other fishes from the tank.

UNDERSTANDING SCIENTIFIC NAMES

Taxonomy is the science of classifying plants and animals. A branch of taxonomy, known as nomenclature, is the naming of living things. All animals, fish included, are given Latin names that appear in italic type. The first name is the genus of the animal. The second is the species name. If one is referring to an entire genus of fish, it is customary to write the genus name followed by the designation "sp" for species, or "ssp" for subspecies.

Some cichlids, like angelfish, are *open breeders,* which means they lay their eggs on a vertical surface and guard them until they hatch. In the aquarium, angelfish may eat their eggs, the wriggling fry or the free-swimming fry, but in the wild, they tend to take better care of their young. Usually, whenever a cichlid eats its young, it's because there is either the need to spawn again or some threat to the fry—from other fish in the tank to poor rearing conditions. It's generally considered abnormal for a cichlid to eat its young, unlike many of the livebearers that are highly cannibalistic and routinely consume the young if they can catch them. Cichlid fry "trust" their parents and view them as the protectors they usually are.

Cichlids are known for their parental care.

Cave breeders lay their eggs in a sheltered place, such as the inside of a flowerpot. Many of the dwarf cichlids choose this method of protecting their eggs. It's very interesting to watch a female guarding the entrance to the cave while the eggs are developing. Then, one day, you will see the female emerge with a swarm of fry swimming close to her—a most beautiful sight!

Mouthbrooders, like mbuna, pick up the eggs after they have been laid and carry them in their mouths until the fry are free-swimming. You can tell that a female cichlid is holding eggs in her mouth because you can see the little eyes through her cheeks. Her mouth will bulge with fry until one day they are released to hover close to her. When danger threatens, Mom opens her mouth, and all the fry rush to the safety of her *buccal cavity.*

These are just a few examples of how cichlids breed. Some are monogamous and remain together as couples for long periods of time. Others are polygamists, or harem breeders, where one male makes the rounds of several females. Whichever type of cichlid you keep, you can be sure of one thing—it's never boring!

chapter 2

Cichlid Behavior in the Aquarium

Behavior is a large part of what makes cichlids such intriguing aquarium pets. No other kind of fish demonstrates the action and interaction of cichlids. Some are bold. Some are smart. Some are powerful. But none are dull. There is a wide range of mannerisms in cichlids, and there are ways to cope with some of the antisocial behaviors.

Not all cichlids pester their tankmates, but it would be a real disservice to both the fish and the aquarist to pretend that aggression doesn't occur. Many cichlid species are exceptionally aggressive, frequently driven by mating instincts. Reproductive strategies figure prominently in cichlid behavior (although they aren't the only forces at work). Other times, cichlids are dangerous to tankmates simply because they view them as food, which is a natural mistake. Remember, though, that there are many cichlids, and each type has its own strengths and weaknesses. (Behaviors of different cichlids are addressed in part three.) Not all cichlids shred plants or break equipment or try to make a meal of the pretty fish you bought to keep them company.

Aggressive Behaviors

Tank Beaters

Slam! Uh-oh. The Oscar is beating up the filter again. Sometimes it seems as though your fish is determined to break every ornament, heater and filter in the tank. It literally trashes the tank every time your back is turned. (Yes, some cichlids will wait until you aren't looking to do their dirty work.) Some fish dig constantly, lifting and dropping rocks on the bottom glass, to the point where there is real danger they could break the tank. Where will that leave them? High and dry; but as smart as cichlids are, they don't understand that if they break the glass, they'll be fish out of water.

SIZE DOESN'T PREDICT PERSONALITY

Size is no indicator of the cichild's temperament. A tiny pair of dwarf cichlids exhibit unmatched fury if their young are threatened. A pair of discus, the most peaceful of cichlids, can damage other discus that try to interfere with their spawning plans—though they would never attack any other species.

It is your responsibility to anticipate the behavior of the fish and create an environment that will either reduce the negative behavior or "fishproof" the tank. If you are a fan of large cichlids that root in the substrate for food or dig spawning pits (such as the eartheaters of the *Geophagus* species), it's not in your best interest to use undergravel filters or have a collection of exotic plants. (*Geophagus* are not hard on the plants themselves, but the digging damages the roots.)

Excavation-minded cichlids uncover the filter plates and make undergravel filters ineffective. Even potted plants are moved around as they redecorate, and plants rooted in the gravel are dug up. Diggers need

large, flat rocks that they can't move and coarse gravel that they can shift to their hearts' content. It helps if you anticipate their actions and use silicone cement to permanently attach rockwork to the bottom glass of the aquarium before any water is added.

Boredom

Some cichlids that wouldn't ordinarily be destructive can become so in confinement simply out of boredom. In the wild, they are accustomed to almost unlimited space and the stimulation of hunting, fleeing and uncertainty. It doesn't take long for them to examine an aquarium of any size and, lacking the normal "work" of being fish, they turn their energies toward destruction.

In a cichlid tank, large, flat rocks that cannot be moved by the fish are recommended (Lobochilotes labiatus).

Tankmates can help correct this problem if the tank is large enough to accommodate them comfortably and there aren't compatibility problems. Another approach is to have two adjacent tanks so the fish can see each other. They are usually too busy staring through the glass to destroy the tank. Situating the tank where the fish can see you also helps alleviate boredom. You will be charmed by the excitement your fish displays whenever you come into sight. These intelligent fish respond to people and make it very clear who they like and who they don't yet know. Some owners use Ping-Pong balls as fish toys, and it's a great pleasure to teach your intelligent fish to respond in certain ways to your signals. Be careful, though, of holding food above the tank for your fish to jump and take the food from your fingers. It is all too easy for the fish to develop a habit of jumping that could land it dead and dried on the floor.

By keeping fish of the same size, you greatly reduce the likelihood of predation in your tank.

Warriors

Predation

Cichlids are famous for predation, which is a simple concept. The predatory fish is hungry. A smaller fish, the prey, is in the vicinity. The fish catches and eats the smaller fish. There's no other motive. Not all cichlids are meat-eaters, but many that are hopeless hunters in the wild, given to eating insects and plants, will, if they can, eat a smaller fish in the aquarium. Generally, if another fish fits in the mouth of a larger fish, it's food. There are exceptions; some species that are mainly vegetarian will not harass even the smallest fish, but they are real exceptions, rarely found among cichlids. The only way to prevent one fish from eating another is to avoid mixing large and small fish in the cichlid aquarium.

Fighting

Aggression is not easily forgiven or understood. If the fish is hungry and eats a tankmate, the aggression is

understandable, but it's baffling when they harass tankmates that don't seem to be causing them any grief. Such behavior is usually associated with territory or feeding rights. The fish that has the territory of its choice is "happy." Along with the territory comes access to food and freedom to mate, thereby greatly enhancing the fish's quality of life.

Male fish usually select and defend territories, but females can also be quite aggressive when there are eggs or young involved. You can easily tell when a fish has selected a territory, whether it's a rock formation, a piece of driftwood or a corner of the tank. The fish chooses a site and "rushes" any fish that swims past, often taking a chunk of fin or flesh.

Two male Firemouths face off—typical cichlid behavior.

When this aggressive behavior is part of the pre-spawning ritual, usually the same species is attacked. When the male has claimed his spawning site and his female(s), he isn't going to take any chances. There is no way another male is going to get a chance at taking his home or his mate. After spawning, however, all other fishes are threats to the eggs or fry, and both the male and the female are quite fierce in defending their young.

One way to avoid mating-related aggression is simply to keep a tankful of males of different species. In the cichlid world, as in much of the animal kingdom, the males are often the more attractive of the sexes, and a mixed species tank of colorful adult males is a sight to behold. When no females are around, the males usually tolerate each other quite well because fighting over breeding sites or females isn't an issue.

Aggression in mbuna, certain cichlids from Lake Malawi known for their ferocity, is diminished by a technique known as *controlled crowding*. In controlled crowding, a large, undecorated tank is somewhat heavily stocked with young mbuna that grow up together. Lacking rockwork or other decorations, there are no territories to defend, so they simply don't have anything to fight about other than food. If you choose this approach, you must make sure your filtration and maintenance routine is top-notch, because you could certainly lose your fish if the water quality went bad.

If you are interested in breeding your fish, you should keep a single pair (except for those species that are polygamous, where the ratio is usually one male to three females) in an aquarium that's right for their size. Depending on the species, there may still be some fighting, and you might want to use a tank divider some of the time; however, cichlid spawning and parental behavior is fascinating to watch and worth the effort.

Given the careful attention paid to fry by adult cichlids, one would think that the young fish could stay indefinitely with the parents. It is rare that this would be successful even among the most peaceful of cichlids. Eventually, the parents will spawn again and at that point, the young of the former spawning will be considered a threat to the new family and will be annihilated. In the wild, the young will wander away from the family group, leaving their parents in peace to spawn again, but in the aquarium it is best to remove the youngsters to be raised independently after the recommended time with their parents.

Finally, there are some fish that don't seem to get along with any other fish. They are simply renegades and must be kept alone. Fortunately, they are often

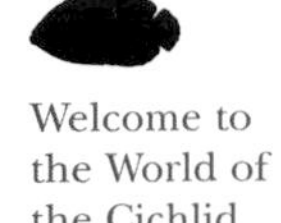

intelligent, interesting and attractive and make excellent pets. Many aquarists wouldn't trade their Managuense or Texas cichlid for a tank full of any other kind of fish.

Shyness

Shyness is not uncommon among cichlids in the aquarium. To give those shy cichlids a sense of security, adding a school of active fish that swim in the open water goes a long way toward bringing your cichlids out into the open. Schooling fish used for this purpose are known as *dither fish.* The theory behind using them is that the smart cichlid figures out that if the dither fish aren't fleeing or being eaten, it must be safe to come out into the open.

For a community tank, it may be best to combine dwarf cichlids with other small species (Apistogramma cacatuoides).

The choice of dither fish depends on the cichlid involved. For dwarf cichlids, almost any small, peaceful schooling fish, such as Cardinal or Neon Tetras, will do, provided they are comfortable in the cichlid's tank conditions. Obviously, they can't be so small that they would be viewed as food, nor so active that they would drive the cichlid crazy or nip at its fins. Rainbowfishes are often used in African cichlid tanks. Large Danios and Barbs are good choices for tanks that contain bigger cichlids, and the largest cichlids are pacified by big, fast fish, such as Silver Dollars.

Compatible Tankmates for Cichlids

Many people just can't wrap their minds around keeping a tankful of only one kind of fish, so they need variety in the aquarium. Tankmates for cichlids are limited. Loricarids are acceptable in most cases. These pleco-type fishes are called "armored catfish" and are well able to withstand all but the most aggressive cichlids. Fishes of similar size as your cichlids may also be suited to life with your fish. (Remember, size is an important factor in combining fishes.) They could include Clown Loaches, Red-Tailed Sharks, Tri-Colored Sharks and Bala Sharks.

Dwarf cichlids, on the other hand, can be kept with almost any other small, peaceful species that requires similar keeping conditions. Favorite tankmates for acid-loving dwarf cichlids are the *Corydoras* species, schools of tetras, angelfish, discus, Hatchetfish and Pencilfish. Nanids, such as *Badis badis,* are ideal tankmates for dwarf cichlids. They are colorful, similarly sized, and peaceful enough to be welcomed into a beautifully decorated dwarf cichlid tank.

FINICKY FISH

Do not be surprised if you see your cichlids doing strange things sometimes. These are very clever fish that have evolved to be "winners." Some of them are just as likely to bury themselves under the gravel when frightened as they are to leap from the water to snatch a treat from your fingers.

Spend Time with Your Fish

Cichlid behavior truly is fascinating and is a large part of enjoying these fish. It's only by quietly watching your fish that you can come to fully appreciate the vast range of their behaviors. Take some time to relax in front of your fish tank.

Cichlids

part two 

in the Home

chapter 3

Setting Up the Cichlid Aquarium

Given cichlids' great variety of size and temperament, no single aquarium arrangement can suit all cichlids all the time.

The Tank

Size

When selecting a tank, the most important consideration is its size. It's critical that the fish you keep are housed in an appropriately sized tank. Nothing is sadder to a fish lover than to see a large cichlid stunted and deformed by being kept in a tank that's too small for it. Don't be fooled by the size of the fish when you buy it. Most cichlids for sale are young specimens. The brightly colored, inch-long *Pseudotropheus* sp. offered in the shop may look lost at first in a 10-gallon tank, but by this fish's first birthday, it should be a chunky 4- or 5-inch fish with a hearty appetite (and these are modestly sized fish by cichlid standards). Granted, a pair of dwarf cichlids, such as Rams *(Microgeophagus ramirezi)*, will do quite well long-term in that 10- or 15-gallon tank, but they are small fish.

Always research the adult size of any cichlid you are thinking about owning, and size the tank accordingly. The correct-sized tank allows two to three gallons for every inch of adult fish. Although much of what you read in the aquarium literature says one inch of fish per gallon of water is permissible, there's a vast difference in body mass between most aquarium fish and cichlids. Cichlids, on the whole, tend to have deep, well-fleshed bodies—and appetites to match.

Determine the size your cichlid will be at maturation, and buy a tank to accommodate it. A Zebra Cichlid, for example, is not a large fish, but it isn't happy living in a 10-gallon tank.

The tank should have as large a bottom surface area as possible. High show tanks are appropriate only for high-bodied fish, such as discus and angelfish. Rectangular tanks are fine, but a tank that sacrifices depth for width is even better. Most cichlids spend little time at the surface and a lot of time patrolling the bottom of the tank. Not only will your fish appreciate a good-sized swimming space, but the more surface area available for gas exchange at the waterline, the better the water quality is in any tank.

Glass or Acrylic?

It doesn't really matter whether the tank is made of glass or acrylic. The choice is yours, but bear in mind

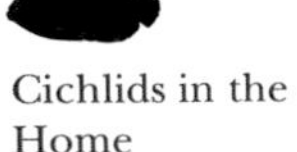

that acrylic is fairly easy to scratch. On the other hand, acrylic's light weight often more than compensates for the delicacy needed when cleaning the surfaces. Some people build their own tanks of plywood fronted with glass and sealed with marine paint. In warmer climates, cichlids are even kept outdoors in ponds or wading pools in the summer. One friend keeps an old bathtub full of African cichlids in his basement. Most people, however, prefer to keep their cichlids in a standard aquarium. It's only when their hobby has expanded beyond their space that they start looking at alternatives.

Surface area is an important consideration when purchasing a tank. The surface-to-air ratio of the tank is much larger than that of a bowl.

TANK TIPS

The following are some basic things to keep in mind when choosing your aquarium tank:

- Choose the largest tank you can afford and accommodate.
- Choose a long rectangular tank instead of a tall one.
- Never use a goldfish bowl.
- Make sure there are no gaps in the sealant.

The Tank Stand

Big tanks are heavy. For example, one gallon of water weighs 8.3 pounds, so you can well imagine the weight of even a 30-gallon tank with water, gravel and other furnishings. Be sure your floor can take the strain before you set up a big tank and fill it with water!

As long as it's absolutely level, the tank can be placed on just about any piece of furniture (except the television!) that will bear the weight and will not be damaged by the inevitable drips.

Many attractive aquarium stands are available in shops, from the standard iron tank stands to cabinets with storage areas, but you can easily construct a perfectly serviceable stand from 2 × 4s or blocks. Above all, the tank must be level. Even a slight unevenness stresses the seams of the aquarium and could result in leaking. If there's any doubt at all, place a sheet of Styrofoam® under the tank.

The Tank Cover

Because cichlids are powerful jumpers, the usual plastic aquarium hood isn't adequate for these fish. A frightened cichlid has enough power to knock that hood right off the tank. A glass cover with only enough space open for the necessary equipment is much better, but some fish can still jump through the space. If you are using a plastic cover, some extra weight on top might help prevent losing fish.

AN ATTRACTIVE WAY TO PREVENT ESCAPES

Floating plants are useful in some cichlid tanks to help stop leapers. When the top of the water is covered with Water Sprite, Duckweed, or Riccia, the fish feel more secure and are less likely to jump out of the tank when startled. If they are being chased, the plants probably won't help, but anything you do to cover the tank lowers the chances of losing fish.

Lighting

Fluorescent tubes are generally used for lighting cichlid aquariums. Because cichlids don't usually care for bright light, a single light in a reflector is a good choice. You want enough light of the quality that shows the fish off to their best advantage, without causing them undue psychological stress. Tubes in the red and blue ends of the spectrum are ideal.

The lights should be left on for 12 to 14 hours a day to simulate the natural light period in the tropics where cichlids are found. An unlit aquarium is not healthful because fish require periods of light and darkness to regulate their circadian rhythm. Lighting cycles assist a fish in knowing when it is time to rest, eat or breed.

Don't count on the sun to illuminate your tank; if you've ever spent a vacation on the beach, you know that sunshine is unreliable. One day it's too hot, and the next day is cloudy. At its best, sunlight occasionally lights up a flash of iridescence on a fish that you might

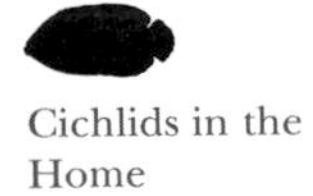

have missed otherwise. At its worst, however, it can cook your fish and stimulate the growth of excessive amounts of unsightly algae.

On the other hand, too little light can cause algae as well: brown algae. Actually, what's called "brown algae" is *diatoms,* but the lack of light usually results in an ugly brown covering over the glass and other surfaces in the tank.

SAFETY FIRST

Let's stop worrying about the fish for a minute and worry about you. Always use a Ground Fault Interrupt (GFI) outlet for your aquarium power. All it takes is one accident with water and electricity, but the GFI helps prevent you from getting shocked. Even with a GFI, however, use caution. Never handle a broken heater without first unplugging it. If you drop a piece of electrical equipment into the water, unplug the unit before you fish it out of the tank.

Aquarium chemicals can be dangerous, too. Keep all water conditioners and medications well out of the reach of children and pets. Keep the fish food locked up as well. The family cat or dog may devour a month's worth of pricey pellets in one quick meal (and will not be glad it did).

Fish may not have eyelids, but they do sleep, so avoid turning on the tank light suddenly. Sunrise is a gradual process. If you want to turn on the light at night, turn on a low room light first and wait until you see your fish start to wake up before turning on the tank light. Some cichlids sleep very deeply—discus are a good example—and if you startle them awake, they'll dash around or even jump out of the tank.

Location

Part of the beauty of cichlids is their intelligence. Compared to most other fishes, cichlids have a keen awareness of their surroundings. A goldfish, for example, might not be disturbed by the activities of a busy family, but count on your cichlids to be aware and probably quite stressed by sudden noises and quick movements. Once your cichlids settle in, they will be just another one of the gang in many cases, but it's best not to let them stay in a panic state.

Place your cichlid tank in a quiet, out-of-the-way place. You can become a part of their world only if they are calm and secure. A frightened fish cowers behind any available cover and certainly doesn't feel safe enough to come to the front of the tank to greet you. Neither you nor your fish will enjoy your life together.

Heat

Cichlids are tropical fishes, so incorrect water temperature is very harmful to them, leading to disease and death. The range of temperatures where they are found is from 70° to the mid-80s°F. Check on the proper temperature for your kind of cichlid, and set the heater to that temperature.

Heaters are essential in most cichlid aquariums; in particular, a heater with a thermostat built in keeps your fish in a safe and comfortable water temperature.

Find a quiet corner for your cichlid tank. These fish can become stressed by noise and activity.

Invest in the very best heater you can afford because inexpensive heaters tend to perform unreliably. Submersible heaters are a better value than those that hang on the side of the tank. You can mount them near the bottom of the tank, which increases the circulation of heated water. It also prevents the warm heater being accidentally exposed to cooler air during water changes, which could result in a broken heater. The glass covering on the submersible heaters also seems to be thicker, which is definitely an asset in a tank of tough cichlids.

Five watts of heater power for every gallon of water is enough to adequately warm the water. However, it's best to use two heaters in large tanks, with each being "responsible" for half the total wattage required.

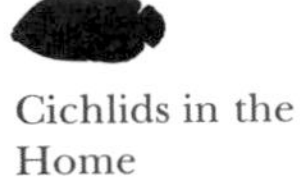

Make no mistake about it: Some cichlids view the heater as the enemy. The bigger cichlids, such as Managuense, Oscars and Jack Dempseys, will certainly do their best to break your heater. You can protect your heater (while the tank is still empty and dry) by taking a piece of PVC pipe with a diameter large enough to insert the heater, drilling several holes in it and adhering it to the back wall of the tank with silicone cement. When you fill the tank, simply slip the heater into the pipe, and the fish can ram it all day without breaking it. You may have to devise similar protectors for the filter intake tube, too, although it might be better to cordon off a corner of the tank with wire mesh or a stable barrier of rockwork for this purpose.

Heater haters, such as the Jack Dempsey, can make maintaining the correct water temperature a challenge. Protect your heater from large, aggressive cichlids with a length of PVC pipe.

You need a thermometer to verify whether the heater is functioning. For cichlids, a thermometer that sticks to the outside of the tank is both convenient and accurate. Check the temperature daily when you feed your fish. When you buy a thermometer, compare its temperature to others in the store display to be sure it's giving an accurate reading.

Substrate

There are many kinds of gravel on the market, and a few are just right for the cichlid tank. For cichlids, you can use a dark or natural-colored sand or small-diameter gravel. Washed river or beach gravel is ideal. Coated epoxy gravels in a wide variety of colors are suitable for a decorative effect, but they are a poor choice if you plan to use an undergravel filter.

If you are keeping hard-water fishes, such as Africans, you can mix the sand with crushed coral gravel. This substance contains calcium carbonate, which helps buffer the water, making it possible to keep the pH high and stable. The best substrate for these tanks is about 3 inches of natural-colored pebbles mixed 50-50 with the coral. The pebbles should be rounded and even in size. Rinse your substrate many times, until the rinse water runs clear. This step saves you the aggravation of watching the filter have to deal with the milky dust.

Be particular with the substrate you choose. Some substrates are simply dirt traps, and others are outright dangerous to your fishes. Avoid the small bits of colored glass you occasionally see offered in stores.

Rockwork

Cichlids enjoy swimming around rocks, but it's best to cushion the glass with silicone cement or Styrofoam®.

Rocks are both decorative and functional in most cichlid aquariums. True, the world is full of rocks free for the taking, but do yourself and your fishes a favor and stick to safe rocks available at your pet shop. Unless you are absolutely certain that the rocks you find in your backyard aren't going to leach toxins into the water, pet shop rocks are far cheaper compared to the cost of replacing a tankful of fishes. Don't place rocks directly on the glass because the pressure points created by a large rock sitting on a piece of sand can crack the bottom glass. You can cushion the glass by layering the projections the rock rests on with silicone cement or by fitting a piece of Styrofoam® under the gravel bed. You can

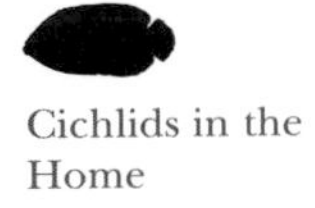

even construct elaborate rockwork structures that feature a front and back door to each cave.

Rocks are great, but they do tend to be heavy. Many people keep cichlids in tanks with few or no rocks at all. As an alternative to rocks, you can sucessfully use lengths of PVC pipe attached to each other with silicone cement. As long as there are hollow spaces and the materials are not toxic, you can use almost any vessel or cylinder to create your cichlid territories.

Driftwood

Driftwood is a valuable addition to the rock piles you construct in your aquarium, but don't use wood you find on the beach or in your local lake. It's quite possible it contains parasites or their eggs, and you just don't know its history. Driftwood that you find outdoors may have been sitting in water contaminated with oil or some other toxin; this would definitely not be good for your fishes. Several safe varieties of driftwood can be found in pet stores.

Driftwood should not be used in alkaline, hard-water tanks. By its very nature, driftwood tends to soften and acidify the water. This is ideal when you're keeping dwarf and South American cichlids, but it's not recommended for African cichlid tanks, where you must keep the pH and water hardness values high.

Backgrounds

The background covering of your tank has quite an impact on the appearance of your fishes, and it plays a large role in how your fishes behave. Cichlids feel vulnerable when there's a lot of space around them. They come out and flash their brilliant colors only when they know they have a safe retreat. Using a natural background—some people go the limit with backgrounds molded from real rocks that a plastic cast is made from—makes your fishes feel safe enough to display their best. They court their females, threaten competing fish and give you a jolly good show when they sense that they aren't entirely exposed.

Filtration

The filter you choose depends on which type of cichlid you're keeping. You can use a standard filter with dwarf cichlids and other lightweight cichlids, but you will need heavy-duty filtration for big, husky cichlids.

Big cichlids have big appetites and are sloppy eaters that produce a lot of waste while they are eating. Their dining habits make it a challenge to maintain the water's chemical and visual quality. If you watch a big cichlid eat, you invariably see a cloud of food pass out through its gills with every gulp. If the meal of the day happens to be feeder goldfish, you can see the shiny scales exiting as well. So much for water clarity.

The term *filtration* is used here in a broad sense to embrace all the processes that help maintain water quality. There are more filtration products on the market than you would believe possible, plus several filtration techniques. When you know the technique—mechanical, chemical, biological and even vegetative (planted tanks)—you can see how waste is removed from the water, which helps you choose the filtration that best serves your purpose for your particular tank.

> **FIND A REPUTABLE DEALER**
>
> Shop around before buying your aquarium equipment. You should find a reputable dealer you're comfortable with who can advise you on how to select equipment that functions successfully as a unit and is right for the fish(es) you will be keeping. Also, you want to know that you can contact the person who sold you the equipment if you have questions or if something goes wrong.

As your hobby expands into different levels, you won't use the same kind of equipment or the same technique for every setup. For example, a 50-gallon show tank uses a different type of filtration than a 50-gallon breeding tank, and you wouldn't necessarily use the same type of sponge filter on two different tanks. As your experience and observations increase, you'll become adept at fine-tuning your choices to suit each situation. This is another fun part of the hobby: You get the opportunity to become opinionated and be an expert.

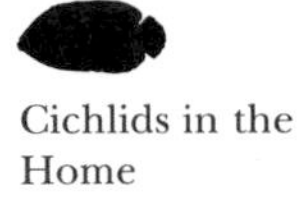

Mechanical Filtration

The main goal of mechanical filtration, also called "pre-filtration," is to remove large floating particles of uneaten food, fish waste and plant waste. There are many ways to do this: sponges, pads, floss—practically any inert mesh-type material that captures the dirt. Simple filter floss is very inexpensive and effective. Depending on the style of filter you choose, the pre-filter medium is situated where the water first enters the filter; you might, for example, use a small sponge on the intake tube of your power or canister filter. Some filters have special chambers for pre-filtration media. Even the old-fashioned box filter with a layer of gravel and some filter floss performs effective mechanical filtration because these materials trap the dirt as the water passes through them.

Mechanical filters must be changed or cleaned weekly, but, unfortunately, many people don't realize this is a necessity! Mechanical filters capture the solid wastes that must be broken down to liquid form before they can be converted by the nitrifying bacteria (a process described in the next section). It's far more practical to simply remove the solid wastes than to wait for them to liquefy and be processed by the biological filter. Removing the wastes helps prevent overtaxing your filtration system, so whichever method of mechanical filtration you choose, keep it clean! This is one area where you don't have to worry about preserving your bacterial bed. Just wash, rinse or replace that mechanical filter medium as often as possible.

Biological Filtration

The Nitrogen Cycle

In the aquarium, beneficial bacteria—known as *nitrobacters*—colonize the biological filter media and every surface of the tank. *Nitrosomonas* sp. is the nitrobacter that consumes the toxic ammonia produced by the decomposition of fish waste and other organic matter. The ammonia is reduced to nitrite, which is consumed by *Nitrobacter* sp. and reduced to nitrate, the least toxic end-product of nitrification. This process is known as the *nitrogen cycle*—the backbone of biological filtration.

These bacteria, amazing in their efficiency, are converters that reduce the toxins, ammonia and nitrite into nitrate. They are absolutely necessary for the aquarium's biological function. You can now find instant bacterial cultures that make it possible to start a new aquarium and stock it with fish immediately. In the past, the filter bacteria had to be "seeded" with gravel from an existing aquarium, or there was a 4- to 6-week wait while the bacteria population became established before the tank could be stocked. The advent of freeze-dried instant bacterial cultures has revolutionized tank setup procedures. No more waiting, and no more losing fish to ammonia spikes in newly set up aquariums.

The Nitrogen Cycle.

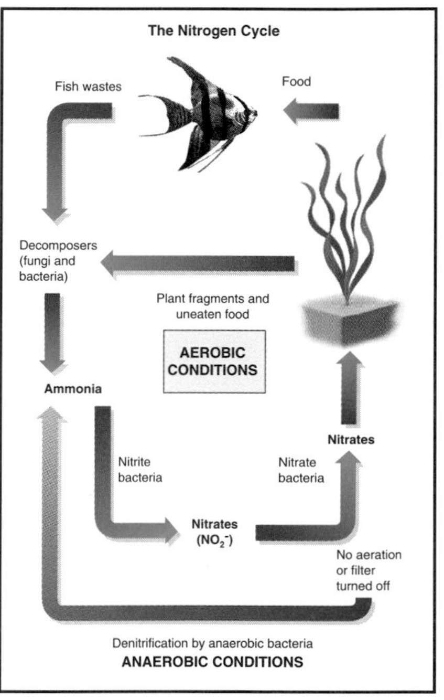

The end-product of biological filtration, nitrate, is removed from the aquarium by your partial water changes, and nitrate-attracting resins are also used to remove nitrate from the aquarium water. This high-tech approach provides excellent insurance against toxic build-up in the aquarium. Mechanical filtration is meant to take particles out of the water—nothing more. Because the same medium is sometimes used for both mechanical and biological filtration, the two are often confused. Biological filtration is that bacterial conversion of nitrogenous compounds described previously in the nitrogen cycle. You want to clean your mechanical filter vigorously and often, but the biological filter performs best when it's left strictly to its own devices with a constant

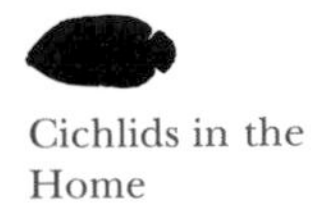

flow of particle-free, oxygenated water through the medium.

There are many types of biological filters. You can use a canister filter, the mainstay of the advanced hobbyist; the trickle filter, which made its bones in the saltwater hobby; the simple box filter, used with tremendous success by experienced fishkeepers reluctant to give up on a filter that has been keeping fishes alive and well for the past 50-odd years; the fluidized bed biofilter, the newcomer on the block; or another kind. Some tanks are maintained for years with nothing more than a simple sponge filter and air pump. Simply squeeze the sponge filter gently in a bucket of tank water once a week, and the resident nitrobacters do a fine job of converting the ammonia and nitrite. But remember that regular siphoning of uneaten food and fish waste goes a long way toward helping you keep a healthy tank when you have a very simple filtration setup.

As many different types of biological filters as there are, there are more types of media. Some examples of biological filter media include plastic hair curlers, "bio beads," gravel, sand, sintered glass (treated with minerals), ceramic noodles and so on. Biological filtration is critical to the health of your fish.

Whichever media you use to harbor your nitrifying bacteria, remember that you want to preserve and protect them. It takes about 6 weeks for the nitrobacters to establish themselves from a standing start in the filter without the benefit of added bacteria. During this critical period, the ammonia and nitrite reach high, perhaps toxic, levels. Keep your fish load very low in the new aquarium, and be careful not to overfeed. A good recommendation is to run the tank with only one or two very small and inexpensive fish during this period. The water may cloud up for a period; this is called *new tank syndrome,* which is normal. The water will clear up as the nitrifying bacteria begin to do their jobs. If you have stocked your tank with "important" fishes, you must check the ammonia level daily until it reaches zero. Partial water changes help keep the ammonia at tolerable levels, but extend the time it takes for the ammonia to reach zero.

To maintain a healthy bacterial colony in the biological part of your filtration system, treat the medium with gentle care. When cleaning it, use only tank water, not hot water or fresh tap water. A gentle rinse with tank water should be all you need to do if you have set up the system properly. The goal is to maintain the bacteria as undisturbed as possible on the medium. It's also a good practice to use a dechlorinator regularly. Chlorine in the water is not only damaging to the gills of your fishes, but also very toxic to the nitrifying bacteria.

If your tank is without power for any length of time, it's entirely possible that your biological filter could crash. This happens when the bacteria are without oxygen for a time period that varies depending on a number of factors; however, if you find that the filter has been off for a day and smells foul, and the fish are gasping for air at the surface, don't simply turn the filter back on! The filter itself has become toxic and must be thoroughly cleaned and the medium replaced before you can use it on the aquarium.

Chemical Filtration

Some tanks do quite well without any type of chemical filtration at all. Frequent small water changes can remove nitrite and other toxins. However, water chemistry varies radically from place to place, and chemical filtration is occasionally necessary simply to keep the fish alive. If, for example, your tap water is very high in phosphate or nitrate, you may find that your fish don't thrive until you pretreat the water with specific resins or activated carbon. It's not within the scope of this book to go into great depth on water chemistry, but be aware that almost any water can be made suitable to keep whatever fishes you want. Water chemistry is a fascinating study, and you might need to become quite adept at water chemistry and water treatment before you can keep any delicate fish successfully. Fortunately,

cichlids are usually quite hardy and withstand a good deal of experimentation as far as their water goes. In most cases, your cichlids are far more likely to suffer from each other's company than from what the water company delivers.

You can create water that's suitable for any type of fish. Members of the genus Crenicichla (Crenicichla johanna), *for example, need softened water.*

Activated Carbon

In granular or powdered form, activated carbon provides one type of chemical filtration. It removes discoloration, dyes, colors, phosphate, chlorine, chloramine, antimony, arsenic, chromium, hydrogen peroxide, potassium permanganate and some of the heavy metals and other toxins in varying degree. It also removes many fish medications at the end of their therapy and is ideal for pre-filtration of tap water to remove most of the residual toxins left after municipal water treatment (and some of the toxins added during water treatment). However, activated carbon does not remove ammonia, nitrite or nitrate, so don't expect it to take the place of biological or mechanical filtration. It does what it does, and it does it well. It should be an integral part of your filtration plan, as long as you understand its properties and its limitations.

Activated carbon adsorbs the above-named toxins. Based on the toxin's concentration in the water, the carbon's effective life span could be a few hours or a few days. Activated carbon is not to be used as a filter medium in biological filters. It is often combined with filter floss and left in the filter indefinitely, but this is *not* the correct way to use carbon. After it has been used to remove toxins from the water, it should not be left in the aquarium to serve as a biological medium. There are other, more appropriate media for this purpose.

Resins

Resins can be compared to magnets: After they are placed in a canister, they attract and then "grab" specific substances, such as nitrate, as the water passes through. There are many different types of resins that capture many substances. Resins have a limited capacity, so they must be recharged when they're saturated. You can choose from different grades of resins, too; some have a long life, and some are exhausted quickly.

Because resins are highly effective, they are used extensively in sophisticated filtration systems; however, if you use resin, you must adhere to a regular schedule of water testing and recharge your resins when they become saturated.

Micron Filtration

Diatom and micron filters are used to capture superfine particles of dirt. The material, either diatomaceous earth or man-made micron filter material, is so dense that even many free-swimming parasites cannot pass through. The use of these materials for fine filtration is excellent for polishing the water.

chapter 4

Aquarium Care and Maintenance

Starting right goes a long way toward keeping a successful aquarium. Take your time. You're probably anxious to see your fishes swimming happily in their new tank, but if you get restless at the beginning, you will have a hard time trying to correct mistakes after the tank is full of water and fishes!

Getting Started

Make a list before you shop for your aquarium supplies. Forgetting something important, like extra airline, can be very frustrating and may delay your work.

Setting up a new tank is relatively easy, but don't begin before you consider the following issues:

1. Make sure you have a convenient water supply. It should be as easy as possible to change water; otherwise, you might be tempted to scrimp on those water changes!

2. After selecting an appropriate aquarium stand, place it in your chosen location, but don't place the stand too close to the wall. On many occasions, you need to work at the back of the tank, and you aren't going to be able to move it easily once it's filled with water. About 8 to 12 inches between the tank and the wall should be enough for maintenance purposes.

3. Rinse your tank with salt and fresh water. Fill it and check for leaks. If you do find a leak at this point, you can easily repair it with silicone sealant.

Fishes are accustomed to getting their light from above. In the confines of the aquarium, light that comes from other directions, especially from below, is very disturbing to the fish, so if you decide not to use a sand or gravel substrate, you should paint the outside bottom of the tank with marine paint. (Many fishkeepers choose bare-bottomed tanks so that they can immediately siphon off leftover food and fish wastes.) Some aquarists, in addition to fully covering the bottom of the tank with rocks and gravel, even paint three sides with an attractive color of dark paint, leaving only the front glass bare to view the fishes. Cichlids feel very secure in this kind of cave-like aquarium.

Set and cement the major rocks into place with silicone if you're using a rock-based arrangement. Select several of the largest, smoothest rocks available and cement them to the bottom of the tank with silicone. Let the silicone dry for 24 hours, and you'll have a good, solid base for further layers of rock. It helps if you draw a diagram of your planned arrangement. Be sure the rocks have no sharp edges. When you've laid

the foundation with the biggest rocks, you can place medium and small rocks toward the front until you get a design that pleases you. Don't set the rocks directly on the glass because the glass could crack where a rock is creating a pressure point.

You will be amazed at how much sediment is carried in new gravel. When you fill your tank, you will be glad you rinsed your gravel well—you won't have to look at so much dust in the water.

Java Fern is a hardy plant that tends to survive uneaten and (sometimes) unmolested.

After you have your rock base and your gravel in the tank, you are then free to arrange the other rocks and driftwood to your liking, always keeping in mind that your fishes prefer places with an entry and an exit. (When you have to net a fish later, you will appreciate your forethought in providing exits to some of the caves. You can just put a net over the exit and drive the fish into the entry.)

Clay flowerpots sliced in half lengthwise are ideal for most cichlid tanks. The material is inert (that is, non-toxic), the color is pleasing and, best of all, each fish can have its own pot.

Plants

If you decide that you want a bit of greenery in your cichlid aquarium, both Java Moss and Java Fern grow on rocks or driftwood, tolerate low light and seem to be unpalatable to fishes. Of course, some cichlids are just interested in destroying plants and not eating them, but it's worth a try. Healthy plants always improve water quality.

It's much easier to put the plants in the tank just before you add the water than to try to get just the right effect when you're up to your elbows in water. At times, it's a bit of a challenge to keep plants with cichlids, but not all of them are deliberately destructive, and many do eat the algae often found on the leaves of living plants. Algae grow on plastic plants, too, so there's no harm in including plastic plants in your decor.

STARTING OFF WITH PURIFIED WATER

It's important to realize that reverse osmosis and deionized water are not used just by people who want soft water. In any area where the tap water is suspected of having toxins in the form of pesticides, heavy metals and the like, it's worthwhile to start with pure water and reconstitute it to the proper chemistry for the fishes involved. Many saltwater enthusiasts, not trusting their water supplies, use purified water to ensure the well-being of their delicate marine organisms.

Adding the Water

Once the tank is decorated and planted, it's time to add the water. A gentle flow of water minimizes the disturbance to your work. You can place a shallow dish in the bottom of the tank and direct the stream of water into the dish to keep the arrangement as you designed it. An alternative is to set a slanted surface, such as a sheet of acrylic over the decor.

After you have added your water, it's safe to turn on your heater and filter without worrying about cracking the glass on the heater or burning out parts of the filter. Remember, it takes about 24 hours for the water temperature to stabilize, depending on the size of the tank and the power of the heater.

Introducing the Fishes

After the tank is set up and running and the biological filtration is in place, it's safe to stock your aquarium. The first stocking of the tank is actually the easiest because subsequent additions are subject to the hierarchies that have formed in the tank.

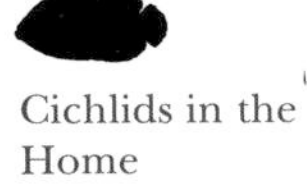

When you bring the fish home from the shop, you can acclimate them easily. Put the fish and the water from the shop into a clean container. Slowly add tank water until the water volume in the container is doubled, and then net the fish into the tank.

Because many cichlids are nervous and stressed when they're moved, the first thing they do when you introduce them to your aquarium is disappear! They immediately take full advantage of your rockwork and stake their claims. However, it won't be long before their natural curiosity is triggered, and you are eye-to-eye with your fish.

By adding water over a slanted surface, you minimize the disruption of your décor.

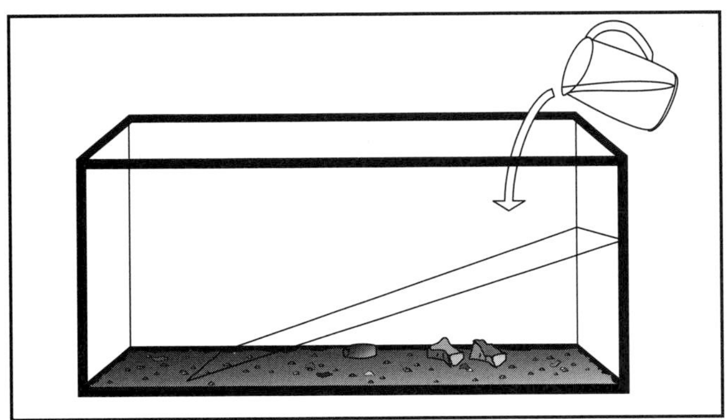

Aquarium Maintenance

When your aquarium is properly set up, maintenance is said to be a relatively simple matter. There must be some fishkeepers who can look at their aquariums without wanting to "fix" something, but I am not one of them. My hobby involves fiddling with my tanks and finding more zen arrangements for the rockwork, which can take as little or as much time as I can justify. But basically, all you really have to do is (1) change 25 to 50 percent of the water every 2 weeks (or in other percentages and frequencies as required), (2) vacuum or stir the gravel and (3) attend to the filter media.

Change Your Water!

The most important aspect of water quality is cleanliness. All the wastes produced by and for your fishes contribute to their discomfort, so it's best if the fish don't have to swim in their own waste. Water changes dilute toxins such as ammonia but do not totally remove it. Fish are very hardy and can often tolerate relatively high levels of toxic waste before they show signs of stress, so you must be on guard not to let the ammonia and nitrite levels rise.

Several factors contribute to the cleanliness of your aquarium water, including keeping a reasonable population of fishes in relation to the size of your tank, not overfeeding the fishes, having an adequate filtration system, using carbon and zeolite in addition to your filter media and frequent partial water changes. It's much better to do frequent small changes than to make infrequent large water changes.

If you have been lax about water changes, be very careful when you do start changing the water again. Your fishes have become accustomed to the high pollution level in the tank, and if you try to mend your ways by doing a massive water change immediately, it could be fatal for the fishes. Don't change a large amount all at once; instead, gradually change the water until it's in good condition. If the fishes are tolerating this well, start to increase the amount of water changed and decrease the frequency of changes until you feel the fishes are looking their best and the water parameters are where you want them to be.

How often and how much water you change depends on many variables, such as how many fishes are in the tank, the type and amount of food offered and the temperature. Just remember that small, frequent water changes are less stressful to your fishes than a large water change. A 25 percent water change once a week is not too much. If you have a heavy fish load in your tank, you may need to change more water than that, but not all at one time. At the very minimum, you should change 25 percent of the water every 2 weeks. If you are keeping delicate fishes, such as discus or some of the dwarf cichlids, you may find that a 25 percent water change every other day is necessary to keep them in peak condition.

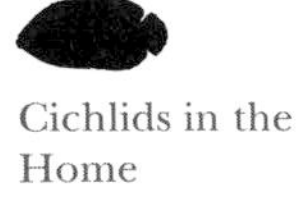

When you do your water changes, be sure to match the water temperature to within a few degrees and add a product that neutralizes chlorine and/or chloramine. Check your pH and add an appropriate product to keep the pH level stable, but make sure you avoid sudden changes in the water's pH.

Remember that water evaporation in your tank affects pH and ammonia levels. As the water evaporates, the minerals, salts, ammonia, nitrates and nitrites remain in the water in greater concentrations, so it's important, if you're not doing a water change, to at least top off the tank regularly to dilute these elements.

To keep more delicate species, you might need to make a 25 percent water change as often as every other day.

Gas Embolism

In cold climates, a gas embolism can occur if you replace tank water with water straight from the tap, and you can lose every fish in your tank if that happens. Cold water can hold more dissolved gases, such as chlorine, oxygen and nitrogen. In the summer, tepid tap water is relatively harmless, except for chlorine and chloramine. In the winter, however, this same water becomes lethal with gas. When the gas-loaded water warms up in your tank (or from the addition of some warm water to bring it to tank temperature), the gas appears in the form of bubbles that cover every surface in the tank—including the fishes. The fish's gills are quite permeable to the dissolved gases, so bubbles can form in their capillaries and cause horrible hemorrhages. Prevention is very simple: Age the water for 24 hours to let the gas escape harmlessly.

Vacuum the Gravel

Changing water alone is not enough to keep your aquarium clean. You will be amazed at the amount of dirt (detritus) that can collect in the substrate. If you were to take a stick and stir the gravel in an established aquarium, you probably wouldn't be able to see the fishes! Every bit of leftover food and fish waste finds its way into the crevices between the stones to decompose at leisure. Bacteria in the substrate breaks down this waste, but it doesn't complete the job, so you have to do your best to maintain a healthy substrate. To do so, vacuum the gravel with a device called a *gravel washer,* a long, thick tube that literally sucks the waste out of the gravel. These devices are great for water changes, and you can even find ones that hook right up to your faucet, clean the gravel, remove the old water, drain the waste water down the sink and add the new water right from the tap. If you're adding tap water, however, be very sure that your water changes are small and that the water chemistry is compatible with the water in the tank.

ANOTHER BENEFIT OF KEEPING GRAVEL CLEAN

By routinely vacuuming the gravel in your aquarium, you help prevent blue-green algae blooms. When keeping fish, you want to encourage the growth of green algae, but the blue-green kind won't impress anyone, not even the fish. Blue-green algae blooms are almost always a sign of *anaerobic conditions,* which are the result of decreased oxygenation, commonly found in areas of the aquarium that have little or no flow of water. Organic material gets trapped in the crevices between the grains of gravel, where it decays, preventing the water from circulating through the gravel. The lack of circulation results in areas of the substrate where oxygen levels are low or absent. This condition eventually becomes toxic to the fishes, but by regular vacuuming, you help keep the water moving through the gravel.

Maintaining Water Chemistry

A good understanding of water chemistry benefits any aquarist. Although you can never absolutely duplicate the fishes' natural environment in the closed system of an aquarium, you can create a hospitable habitat in

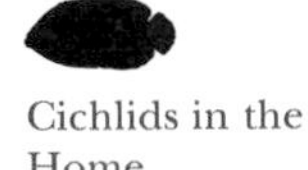

which your pets will thrive and multiply. To fully enjoy an aquarium, you must provide an environment that's compatible with the needs of the particular species you are keeping.

What Is pH?

Two large and important groups of chemical compounds are acids and bases. Water (H_2O or H-OH) is both an acid and a base because, as its chemical formula indicates, pure water has equal concentrations of H+ (hydrogen) and OH- (hydroxide ions). When the concentrations of those two ions are equal, a substance is called *neutral.* An acidic substance contains more hydrogen ions than hydroxide ions. The opposite condition, more hydroxide ions than hydrogen ions, makes a substance a base. Whether a compound is an acid or a base is indicated by its *pH,* or "power of hydrogen," which represents the amounts of acid or base in a solution. Pure water is neutral, so it registers 7 on the pH scale, which ranges from 1 to 14. Below 7, the lower the reading, the more acidic a solution is; above 7, the higher the reading, the more basic a solution is. For example, the pH of lemon juice is about 2.3, which is acidic; the pH of seawater is about 8.3, which is basic.

The responsible hobbyist makes every effort to provide a clean environment fish will thrive in. For example, the Altum Angel (Pteropyllum altum) *likes a deep tank and will not tolerate poor water quality.*

Factors That Affect pH

In the aquarium, the pH of the water naturally goes up and down (called "pH bounce"), even though the owner may have done absolutely nothing to it. How can that happen? Given that the pH changes all on its own, it should be obvious that your actions are going to affect the water chemistry in the tank, too—for better or worse.

The nitrogen cycle responsible for that wonderful biological filtration that eliminates ammonia (a base) is actually creating acid as a by-product. In the aquarium, ammonia is always being produced through the decomposition of waste: feces, urine and the products of respiration, leftover foods and dead things, such as plants, snails and fish. Biological activity in a cycled aquarium converts this ammonia into nitrite and nitrate, which in turn uses up oxygen and produces acid that lowers the pH of the water. In water with a low pH, the ammonia assumes a non-toxic form, called *ammonium,* so it's relatively harmless until you wake up, check your pH, find it alarmingly low and perform a massive water change with water of a higher pH. The ammonia is now liberated! Ammonia is weakly alkaline, or basic, so as it's freed up by the higher pH water, it increases the pH of the water even more, thus converting more ammonium into ammonia, and so on. This is how what you'd normally think of as a healthy water change can actually increase the ammonia level and the pH in the water. But, but, but . . . we all know that water changes are good for fishes! Actually, small, regular water changes are good for fishes because they help to maintain a pH balance. Large, infrequent water changes can precipitate disaster in two ways: ammonia toxicity and the stress of a large, rapid change in the water's pH.

In soft water conditions—water with low mineral hardness—the pH can also drop rapidly. Carbonate hardness "buffers" pH and helps prevent acidification of the aquarium water. Buffers are designed to keep pH at the desired level. They do not change the pH in and of themselves but help keep the pH stable. If you want to maintain a high pH, perhaps for livebearers or African cichlids, and have soft water, you must add some buffering agent to the water. Often this buffer is sodium bicarbonate—good old baking soda. There are many proprietary formulas on the market that make it easy to buffer water without guessing about quantity and method.

Monitoring pH

The simplest way to check your pH is with the dip-and-read type of test strips, which are adequate for

"normal" pH water. As with most pH tests, color changes indicate the pH level. They are fast and accurate enough for most purposes. One benefit is that you use a test once, read the result in a few seconds and throw it away. There's practically no chance of unknowingly spreading disease in multiple tanks.

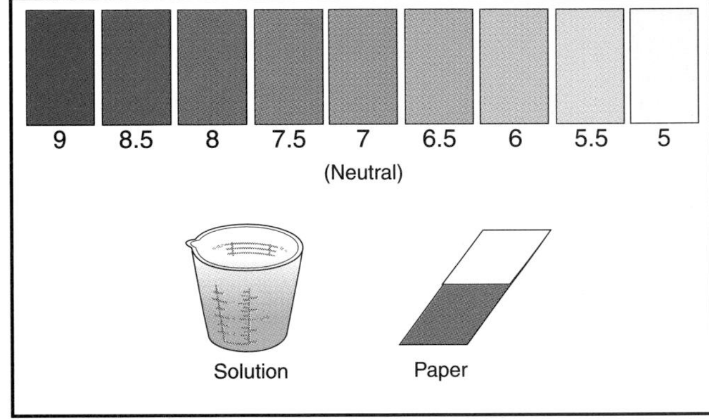

Determining the pH of the water in your aquarium can be done with simple testing kits available at pet stores. Results may look something like this.

Other types of tests, liquid drops or tablets, are available, too, and may be necessary if you need more precise readings at very high or very low pH levels. There are high- and low-range test kits that give results at the extreme end of these values; you might need them if you are keeping fishes that need extremely acidic or alkaline water. The biggest drawback to using drop- or tablet-type pH tests is inconvenience. It takes a little time, and you need a flat surface to work on. (Believe me, a water-protected table near the aquarium is a real bonus in fishkeeping. Many times you find yourself one hand short when you're caring for your fishes, and a flat surface to place your gear on is indispensable.) Electronic pens and monitors are valuable if you are working with fishes that need to be kept at fairly precise pH levels, such as the more delicate African and South American fishes. This equipment is relatively expensive but remarkable for its convenience and accuracy. It's really a must for people who are fine-tuning their water preparation methods and must check the pH levels often.

Changing pH

Any adjustments you make to pH levels should always be initiated outside the aquarium. A change in pH of more than .2 is highly stressful on the fishes, even if it's bringing the water into a more desirable pH for the fishes' natural requirements. A reduction in pH is less stressful than an increase at any point, so when you're increasing the pH level, it's critical to follow the two-tenths of a point rule. Remember the ammonia problem in higher pH water? It's always better to test your methods outside the aquarium than to lose your fishes. To do this, you can use a "fish-only" bucket. Fill your bucket from your usual water source, and add an appropriate amount of either pH increaser or decreaser, stir and then test for results. The amount of chemical you plan to use might need to be increased or decreased, depending on your water supply, and it's far better to use a bucket than your tank to make this determination. Even so, aerate the water and wait 24 hours to see if the reading remains the same.

The most common chemical for increasing the pH level of aquarium water is sodium bicarbonate. Usually, you make a solution of baking soda and water and then add it in very small amounts until the water reaches the desired pH level. The baking soda helps buffer the water as it increases the pH.

ACIDOSIS AND ALKALOSIS

Keeping fishes in water that is either too acidic or too alkaline for their specific biology results in acidosis or alkalosis. A discus, for example, would suffer from alkalosis in high pH water or acidosis in extremely low pH. An African cichlid would likewise suffer from acidosis in low pH water but could also suffer alkalosis in extremely high pH water, even though it prefers a high pH environment.

Fish suffering from acidosis show gill damage and blood chemistry changes. Fish suffering from alkalosis also show corrosion of the gills and fins, and the skin and eyes become cloudy.

To correct either of these conditions, very slowly change the water until the tank water has returned to normal. I add 2 tablespoons of common salt per 10 gallons to alleviate gill and skin damage and reduce nitrite toxicity.

You can usually decrease the pH of aquarium water by adding acids to the water. Very diluted solutions of phosphoric and hydrochloric acid are two chemicals commonly used to reduce the pH level of aquarium water for acidophilic (acid-loving) fishes. Monobasic

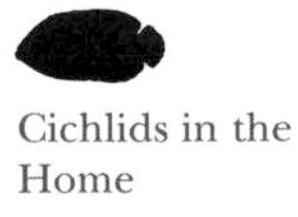

sodium phosphate, which is much safer and easier to find, is also used. In some cases, using phosphoric acid can cause a problem, especially when the source water is high in phosphate. The phosphates can cause algae blooms.

Peat moss is often used to reduce pH and soften water, especially for rainforest fishes. It's usually placed in a bag in the tank or filter, and it gradually tints the water, softens it and acidifies it. There is no "set" amount to use or data available on when to change the peat. When I use peat, I place about 1 or 2 quarts into a nylon stocking that I place into the barrel I use for aging and aerating water. When the pH stops being reduced from my normal tap water level of 7.2, I change the peat.

Sometimes your pH levels seem to be very stubborn. If you have added acid to the tank and the pH has not decreased, you might need to soften your water, too. The water's buffering capacity is resisting your efforts to reduce the pH chemically, so it doesn't do much good to keep adding acid in the hopes of magically arriving at the desired pH level. It's much better to reduce the alkalinity with water that has been softened with an ion-exchange resin, reverse osmosis or distillation. Continuing to add acid to hard water ultimately results in a "crash," and you will find the pH level has dropped far below the comfort level of both you and your fishes.

When you're adjusting the pH level, the aim is to find a routine based on your particular situation—and stick to it.

Water Hardness

We've all heard references, usually on laundry detergent commercials, to hard and soft water, but it's only recently that the aquarium hobbyist has begun to pay close attention to water hardness as a factor that can affect the aquarium's overall water chemistry. Before, it was sometimes a matter of hit-or-miss whether certain species could be kept or bred.

If the local tap water was hard, the aquarist was "lucky" with rift lake cichlids; if it was soft, the aquarist had a "knack" for keeping killies. Whole groups of fishes were dismissed as too delicate or difficult based on the local water's hardness or softness, with the aquarist never realizing that some simple steps could have easily disproved these beliefs. When the body of knowledge about fishkeeping and water chemistry expanded to include water hardness as an important part of the whole, the number of species aquarists could keep successfully increased dramatically.

The total hardness of water is the measurement of dissolved mineral salts, particularly calcium and magnesium. Sodium, potassium and a few others are also present, usually in trace amounts. The hardness of your water is a product of geology (and evaporation, rain, gases in the air and the like). It's also determined by human intervention: Water companies often alter water chemistry for the common good, and aquarists sometimes use calciferous ornaments and gravel without realizing the impact they have on the water chemistry. Geologically, water is hard or soft on the basis of the chemical composition of the area the water travels through on its way to your tap. If you live in a mountainous area or use well water, you can be pretty sure your water is hard. If you live in a rural area on a particular island known for its peat bogs, you can count on your water being soft.

Hard water is suitable for rift lake cichlids, such as Tropheus duboisi, *but you can alter water hardness to meet the needs of your fish.*

Measuring Hardness

There are two types of units of measurement used for total, or general, hardness. In the United States, hardness of water is generally measured in parts per million (ppm). Aquarium and other scientific literature,

however, often uses dH (Deutsche Hartgrad), which means hardness gradient. There are 17.8 ppm in each dH.

Measurements of Total Hardness

dH	ppm	Level of Hardness
0–1.5	0–30	Very soft
1.5–5.5	30–100	Soft
5.5–14.0	100–250	Hard
Over 14.0	Over 250	Very hard

Most people use a drop-type test to measure total hardness, but there are also tablet test kits and dip-and-read strips. With the drop tests, a specific amount of water is poured into a marked vial, and the reagent solution is added, drop by drop. The first few drops turn the water red, and the test is complete when the water turns blue. The number of drops needed to turn the water blue is equal to the total hardness reading of the water sample. Testing methods and the manner of reading tests vary, so please be sure to read and follow the manufacturer's instructions carefully.

Total hardness, the overall hardness of the water, has a direct influence on the life processes of the fishes and plants in the aquarium. Inappropriate hardness levels don't cause sudden death in the same way that extremes of pH do, but in the long term, they can slowly break down a fish's vital systems. In the short term, aquarists might notice that eggs fail to hatch or fry die off shortly after hatching.

Carbonate Hardness

To make things a little more interesting, let's take a look at carbonate hardness, or *alkalinity,* which is a big part of the water chemistry equation, and perhaps more active than total hardness in the way it directly influences the water's pH level.

Alkalinity is the measurement of the bicarbonate and carbonate ions in the water. These ions can come from three sources: by-products of nitrification, mineral carbonates (bicarbonate, carbonate and hydroxide) and carbon dioxide in the water. The amount of these ions in the water, referred to as *total alkalinity,* is expressed in ppm of carbonate (KH). Note that *alkalinity* and *alkaline* may sound similar but, in fact, are different terms and cannot be used interchangeably. *Alkaline* is the word used to describe pH over 7.0.

Many fishkeepers seek to soften their water for specialized species, but it's important to maintain the proper level of carbonate hardness. The buffering effect of carbonate hardness keeps the water at a stable pH value. In water with little or no carbonate hardness, the pH can drop very low very quickly. For good buffering capacity, the alkalinity, or carbonate hardness, should range between 120 and 250 ppm. Starting your aquarium with appropriate carbonate hardness doesn't guarantee stable pH throughout eternity, but it's clearly the method of choice, and your observations based on test results can help you predict when and how much attention your water needs to remain at an acceptable pH level.

Water Hardness and pH

If the pH in the aquarium is too low, you can raise it by using strong aeration to drive off the carbon dioxide or by adding dolomite, crushed oyster shell or sodium bicarbonate. Pet shops carry an almost unlimited array of products designed to buffer the water and adjust pH, either up or down. However, it is advisable to have a good understanding of why the pH level is high or low so that you can choose the best method of maintaining the correct pH. If the pH is dropping because you haven't changed the water for some weeks, it's far better to change your maintenance habits than to add chemicals that wouldn't otherwise be required.

In areas with naturally low alkalinity, the water's pH is easily adjusted initially but tends to drop quickly. To stabilize the pH level, you need to buffer the water chemically. The buffers don't usually change the pH in and of themselves but enable the aquarist to make

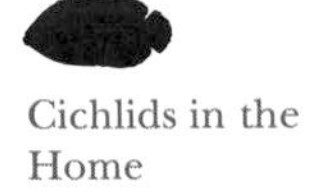

changes in the pH that remain in effect until the carbonate has been depleted.

Softening Water

Where high alkalinity is present, the pH is difficult to adjust in the beginning but generally stays where you put it unless, again, the aquarium is neglected and the carbonates are used up. You might even need to partially soften the water in very hard water areas to produce any change in pH level. On a small scale, you can easily do this by adding distilled water to the aquarium. Distilled water contains no minerals at all, so adding it to the existing water dilutes its mineral content.

Keep the water soft for success with discus.

For those people who are interested in keeping softwater fishes and whose water is naturally hard, there are several options: peat filtration, reverse osmosis, deionization, resin pillows . . . or, of course, moving your house.

Because of the quality of the end product (90 percent pure water by most accounts), reverse osmosis is considered the "best" way to soften water. It may not, however, be the "best" demineralization process under your circumstances. In reverse osmosis, the water is forced by pressure through a semipermeable membrane that traps minerals, bacteria and other impurities. A little research can help you decide which type of membrane and how many gallons per day you need if you elect to use reverse osmosis for your fishkeeping success.

If you choose to use reverse osmosis water, the water must be reconstituted to an acceptable degree of hardness and trace elements for the fishes you're keeping. Pure reverse osmosis water does not contain any minerals or trace elements, and even fishes that live in the softest water need some. This pure water tests neutral for pH and 0 for total hardness and carbonate hardness. To reconstitute reverse osmosis water, some people either add back an appropriate amount of tap water (usually about 15 percent), make up their own formula or use a commercial formula that comes with directions.

Deionization also produces very good-quality water, but there are a few drawbacks to this process: (1) the expense of replacement resins and (2) the danger involved in recharging them. In deionization, the water is passed through resins that attract and hold the minerals and other impurities in the water. Again, if you're using deionized water, appropriate amounts of minerals and trace elements must be added back to the water.

Water-softening resin sachets or pillows, available from several manufacturers, are useful and effective. These small bags contain resins that attract the minerals and replace them with sodium ions.

Peat moss treatment, another method of softening and acidifying water, is certainly the least expensive method and probably the most natural. Driftwood, too, softens the water in the aquarium over time. Peat is available at any garden supply store, either by the cubic yard (a lot!) or in pelletized form (Jiffy-7®). Some hobbyists suggest using Canadian peat moss, but any kind is fine as long as it has not been treated with any kind of fertilizer or pesticide. To test it, place a small amount of peat in a cup of water and, 24 hours later, test for nitrate. If the test is negative, the peat is safe to use.

Hobbyists who use "make-up" water usually designate a new 32-gallon plastic trash bin for their water-conditioning activities. This is an effective way to prepare your water, whether it's to be soft or hard. An airstone and a heater will serve you well (as long as you keep the heater from melting the plastic); aeration and heat remove many of the toxins (particularly chlorine) from raw tap water. If you're using peat, it's a simple

matter to fill a nylon stocking with peat and leave it in the barrel until the water reaches the desired pH level. Granted, the peat tints the water a light amber color, but it's clear, and the shade accentuates the colors of the fish. It's remarkable how rainforest fishes react to this water treatment regimen. If you want to use the peat in your tank, the method is essentially the same: Use about a quart of peat in a nylon stocking and replace it periodically.

Note: Never use a laundry water-softening product in the aquarium, and never use water produced by a water-softening system for the entire house. The latter is unacceptable for fish because it replaces the calcium and magnesium with sodium ions, which are unhealthy for freshwater fishes.

Hardening Water

If you want to harden your water, as for rift lake cichlids, you must pay close attention to alkalinity. If your KH is low, add commercially prepared buffers, sodium bicarbonate (baking soda) or calcium carbonate, or use dolomite or crushed oyster shell. One teaspoon of baking soda per 10 gallons of water is usually enough, but test the water after aeration to determine your own recipe.

In high pH systems, give special attention to aeration and ammonia. Aeration drives off the carbon dioxide that lowers the pH level, and ammonia is considerably more toxic (and more available) in high pH water.

Routine Maintenance Will Become Routine

Maintaining a stable aquarium environment can be a challenge, even for experienced aquarists. The best advice I can give you is to identify the preferred keeping arrangements for your particular fishes: water chemistry, temperature, food type, tank layout and compatibility. From there, you can develop a routine maintenance plan that will become (semi) automatic over time.

Maintenance Checklist

Test the water for pH, ammonia and nitrite weekly in the first six months; after that, check pH, nitrite and nitrate biweekly or when you suspect a problem. Other tests may be necessary depending on your water chemistry or the type of fish you are keeping.

Change 10 to 50 percent of the water weekly. How much water you change and how often you change it depends upon the volume of the tank, number of fishes, size of the fishes and your feeding habits.

Siphon the gravel. Some aquarists routinely siphon after every feeding. Siphon the gravel at least with every water change. Sometimes siphoning can permit a short delay in water changing.

Clean the glass inside and out at least once a month. If you have an algae problem, you may need to clean the inside glass more frequently. Periodically clean the inside of the light cover.

Check the filter with every water change. Change or rinse the media as recommended by the manufacturer.

Clean the inside of the lift-tubes of the filter. Change any air line or flexible hose that has become discolored or stiff. Minerals build up on the inside of the hoses and reduce water flow tremendously.

chapter 5

Selecting Cichlids

After you choose a tank and you're thinking about which kind of cichlids you would like to keep, make a list of the ones actually available to you. We all have "wish fish" we have seen in books and magazines but that we may never see "in the scales." Not every fish is available in every pet shop in the land. Shops carry only what they can keep well and what they can sell. If you're lucky, you have a good pet shop near you that has an interesting selection of fish. Many people mail-order fish with great success, and you can certainly expand the selection by getting to know breeders and other serious aquarists. All the aquarium magazines carry advertisements for exotic fish breeders. Mail-ordering fish is not nearly as risky as you would imagine; they do travel well.

Do Your Homework Before You Buy

Make your own fish wish list, including compatible species you would like to see in your tank. Find out as much as you can about each fish before you start shopping. In addition to the information in part three of this book, review other aquarium books and magazines for information about the different species and their peculiarities. Other aquarists and breeders are usually more than happy to tell you about the individual traits of their favorite fish. When you feel you know the fish well, it's time to shop.

Examine the Fish Closely

When you do find a fish you want, look it over carefully. Cichlids may not always be in top form in a dealer's tank. They have certainly been traveling recently and might not be in a situation entirely to their liking, but they shouldn't look beat up or skinny.

Look for fish with full, intact fins, like this Leopard Angelfish.

The eyes should be clear and intact. Opacity of the eye can result from a simple abrasion, or it might be a bacterial infection that causes the fish to lose the eye. The eyes should not be sticking out. Protruding eyes could be indicative of popeye, a condition that's seldom cured. Many cichlids have slightly protuberant eyes—it makes them very expressive—but avoid any fish with eye damage.

All the fins should be present and intact. Minor fraying of the fins could simply be the result of a bit of recent rough handling, but missing fins or stumps are difficult to manage.

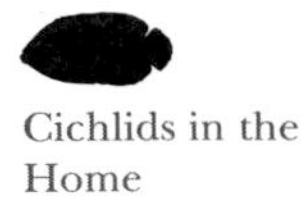

Is the fish's attitude what you would expect? Cichlids are alert and involved in interacting with you and their environment. Don't select a fish that's hiding while all its tankmates are out in the open. Listless fish are not well. If you can, observe the fish eating. If it looks healthy and shows good appetite, it's probably a good buy. If it refuses to eat, it may not be in the best of health.

Have some mental image of the common fish diseases, such as ich, velvet, pop-eye, bacterial infection and the like. (See chapter 7, "Cichlid Health," for more information on disease.) If the fish is covered with spots, has open wounds or shows any other obvious symptoms, it could lead to endless problems in your tank.

Bringing Your Cichlid Home

When you purchase your cichlid, find out as much as you can about the water conditions of the dealer's tank. Even though you have decided to keep your angelfish in the soft, acidic water this species naturally prefers, your dealer might have been keeping the fish in neutral water. When you bring the fish home, match the water chemistry the fish has been kept in as closely as possible, and then gradually bring it into line with ideal conditions.

chapter 6

Feeding Cichlids

Cichlids are usually the easiest of fish to feed. Very few cichlids are picky eaters, but if they are, that usually means they're not feeling well. Cichlids are known for their good appetites and will even consume tankmates if the opportunity presents itself. Many acceptable foods are available in pet shops, but since the greatest fun of keeping cichlids is feeding them, you might want to try some live and homemade foods, too.

Live Foods

There are many advantages to feeding live foods to your cichlids. They are the natural diet of many aquarium fishes, who look and feel their best when live food is included in their diets. Cichlids enjoy live

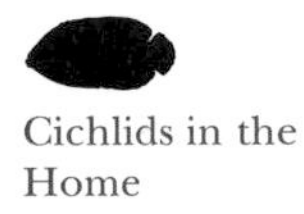

foods, which means much less chance of waste and uneaten food floating around the tank. This reduces the stress on your filtration system and helps prevent water quality problems.

Feeder Fish

The large predatory cichlids, such as Oscars, Managuense and Jack Dempseys, will certainly eat other fishes. Most pet shops have a section of "feeder fish" set aside for just this purpose. For bigger cichlids, choose feeder goldfish; for smaller cichlids, guppies are the best choice. A disadvantage to offering feeder fish is the risk of disease. The feeders may be kept in very crowded or unsanitary conditions, and occasionally, you can see signs of some diseases in the tank. If the feeders don't look healthy, don't buy them. Some cichlid keepers also breed other kinds of fishes and feed a portion of them to their cichlids.

Guppies are a good feeder fish for smaller cichlids.

No doubt, the use of live fish as food for cichlids brings out their interesting instincts. It's much like seeing your fish in its natural environment when it stalks and snaps up its prey. Not surprisingly, some wild-caught cichlids eat nothing but live fish until they are trained to a new diet.

Earthworms

The earthworm is a perfect food for any fish, with the exception of some herbivores, such as *Tropheus,* that can't tolerate a diet high in protein. Earthworms do vary in size, so try to match the size of the worm to the fish you're feeding. Some fish eat them chopped, but it may take a while before they learn to accept the chopped worms. It's better to use a smaller worm that can be eaten in one bite. Sometimes two fish fight over an earthworm, each with one end of the worm in its mouth, tugging for all it's worth!

Almost all cichlids eat earthworms—and you may be able to dig them up in your own backyard!

It's easy to keep earthworms available to feed your fish. Fill a large, plastic storage box (almost to the top) with one-half peat moss and one-half potting soil. Moisten the soil so that it's damp but not soaking wet. You can get small worms from the garden or order them from a garden supply house. The smallest worms are often sold under the name "red wrigglers," and they are ideal for fish feeding. Place the worms in the box. You can feed the worms with cornmeal or bread and vegetable scraps from the kitchen. Stir the leftover food into the soil occasionally to keep the surface from getting moldy. Keep the lid closed when you are not working with the worms. Do not let the worm culture dry out completely, or you'll lose your worms. Earthworm cultures can be kept inside or outside in a shaded location during the summer and should be kept from freezing in the winter.

Adult Brine Shrimp

Live adult brine shrimp (*Artemia* spp.) are treats for all cichlids under about 5 or 6 inches long. They are too small to be of much use to larger cichlids, but angelfish, discus, African cichlids and dwarf cichlids find them delightful.

Live brine shrimp are available in portion containers in many pet shops. You can hatch brine shrimp eggs and grow the young yourself, but the process requires a good deal of time and space.

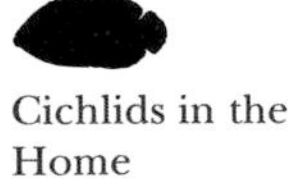

Tubificids: Blackworms and Tubifex

It's with some reservation that I include these two types of worms, and I do so only because they are so often fed to fishes. Both blackworms and tubifex worms are very high in protein and well accepted by small- to medium-sized cichlids. The danger in feeding these worms comes from their generally being found in dirty water and often infected with bacteria and parasites. If you're going to use tubificids, you must rinse them often in fresh water and remove the dead worms.

Feed the worms to the fish with a worm feeder, a floating device with small holes that permit a few worms to crawl through at a time. The fish are ready and waiting for the worms as they escape. Placing the worms directly in the water allows them to tunnel into the gravel, where they will die and pollute the water. Feed only small amounts of tubificids, infrequently and for a certain purpose, such as to encourage a new fish to eat or to condition the fish for breeding.

Whiteworms

Whiteworms are small worms (up to 1 inch long) that are very good for all fish up to about 6 inches long. Larger fish won't bother with them.

Whiteworms can be cultured in a covered plastic shoebox or similar container filled with an equal mix of moist peat moss and potting soil. The soil should be moist enough that it clumps together when squeezed in the hand. Add your starter culture of whiteworms, which you can get from some pet shops or mail-order sources in the tropical fish hobby magazines. Feed the worms white bread, flake fish food or oatmeal mixed with a little milk. Keep the worm culture in a cool place because whiteworms expire at temperatures over 70°F.

Whiteworms are rich and fatty, so use them only as occasional treats or to condition fish for breeding. Again, use a worm feeder to keep the worms available to the fish until they are eaten.

The creatures mentioned in these sections are but a few of the live foods your fishes will relish. Don't be afraid to experiment. If the fish won't eat it, you can always remove the live food from the aquarium. Larger cichlids will take mealworms from time to time, and smaller cichlids will feast on mosquito larvae, bloodworms and glassworms.

Frozen Foods

Almost every pet shop has a freezer with an array of frozen foods, such as bloodworms, frozen brine shrimp, beef heart, various shrimps, krill and other preparations. Give your cichlids a treat and experiment with different frozen foods.

Rinse and thaw frozen worms and shrimps before you offer them to your fishes. Just place a portion in a fine-meshed net and hold it under warm, running water for a few moments. Dinner's ready!

Flake and Other Prepared Foods

Commercially prepared foods—flake, stick, tablet, wafer and pelleted—are undoubtedly the most popular fish food with hobbyists. Fish food manufacturers prepare special diets for all types of fishes and pay careful attention to the amount of protein, fat, fiber, vitamins and minerals that different fishes require.

Select a prepared food that's appropriate for the needs of your fish.

Choose the size and type of food that's appropriate to the fish. A small-mouthed discus will not eat a large pellet, and a big-mouthed tank buster is going to waste a lot of flake food. Prepared foods are available in the correct size and nutritional content for your kind of cichlid. Most prepared foods absorb a lot of water and should be soaked for a few moments before being offered to the fish. If the fishes are greedy eaters and ingest too much dry food too quickly, it swells in their

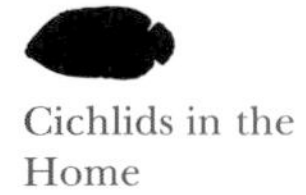

stomachs and causes some considerable distress until it is digested.

Home Cookin'

Your cichlids are almost always ready for a meal, and often your own refrigerator is a good place to find supper. Most cichlids eat just about any kind of *lean* meat. Fatty meats, even hamburger, leave a grease-slick on the water that's quite unsavory in the tank. Strips of lean beef, liver and chicken, cut to the correct size, will be quickly snapped from your fingers by larger cichlids. These meats are perfectly healthy foods for carnivorous cichlids, as long as you trim off all the fat—and watch your fingers!

Lean meats are a favorite of carnivorous cichlids, such as Nissen's Dwarf Cichlid (Nijssen's nijsseni).

For algae-loving fish like mbuna, it's easy to culture algae-covered rocks to simulate their natural feeding habits. You can keep a steady supply of them available year-round for their dining pleasure. Simply place a few rocks in a jar of water on a sunny windowsill. When the rocks are covered with bright green algae, place the rocks in the tank and watch your fish in action. Other foods that can be offered to herbivores include small bits of Romaine lettuce, shelled peas and zucchini. Spinach is also a good food, but do not feed it to your fish every day. Spinach contains oxalic acid that blocks the body's use of vitamin C and leads to deficiency disorders if it's eaten too frequently.

To make homemade paste food, which is very good for meat-eaters, use equal parts of well-trimmed beef or veal heart, liver, shrimp and shelled peas. Cut the meat into small cubes and blend in a food processor with a little water and a few drops of fish or bird vitamins until it forms a putty-like paste. This food can be frozen flat in plastic bags until needed. To feed, just break off a portion, let it thaw a bit and toss it into the tank.

Feeding Your Fishes

Aquarium fishes should be fed small portions several times a day. What constitutes a "small portion" depends on the kind of fish you're feeding. To determine the correct amount, observe how much your fish eats in 10 minutes. After 10 minutes, siphon off any remaining food. If you make this a standard practice and perform regular water changes, your water quality should always be excellent.

Young, growing fish need more frequent feedings than mature fish. Depending on the age and size of the fish, you can vary the number of feedings from two to four or even more per day.

In addition, frequent feeding helps reduce aggression. If your cichlids are hungry all the time, they pounce on any fish that crosses their paths. If they are sated and know that another meal is coming soon, they are less likely to take out their frustrations on a tankmate.

Make sure all the fish get a fair share. If some fish are getting chased away from the food, try distracting the bully with a portion and placing the bulk of the food in another location.

HEARTY APPETITES

Cichlids tend to be good eaters, so you should have no trouble finding foods they enjoy. A fish that isn't eating is apt to be feeling poorly. Keep a close watch on your fishes when you feed them to make sure each one is eating well.

chapter 7

Cichlid Health

It's rare to find a fish in nature that's completely without parasites. Disease-causing organisms and parasites can be found in practically every body of water, whether it is a lake or an aquarium. In a healthy aquatic environment, there's a balance that prevents the disease from overwhelming the fishes' natural resistance. When this balance is lost—whether from the stress of capture and transport, chilling, overheating or water-quality problems that influence the immunity of the fish—the fish is no longer able to resist infection.

Fortunately, cichlids are, on the whole, hardy and vigorous fishes. When they are kept properly, they rarely become sick, but when they do fall ill or have been injured in some way, they need help, and delays can be life threatening.

A Healthful Environment Keeps Your Fishes Healthy

When sick, dying or dead fish are discovered in the existing aquarium, water quality is always the first checkpoint. Test for irregularities of temperature, ammonia, nitrite, nitrate, pH and so on. Often, all that's required to bring the fish back to good health is an upgrade in the maintenance department.

TANK MAINTENANCE IS THE KEY

Many highly contagious fish diseases are introduced by new fish. However, whether diseases actually break out depends on the resistance of your fish. Poor living conditions weaken your fishes, cause chronic stress and ultimately lower their resistance. Maintaining a healthy aquarium goes far toward keeping your fish feeling and looking great!

Ask yourself if the tank has become overcrowded. The fish may have grown beyond the reasonable capacity of the tank and filtration system without your having noticed.

Have some of the fish become more aggressive with maturity? Sometimes peaceful fish turn into tank terrors when they come of breeding age, and the other fish can be seriously injured in territorial disputes.

Quarantine

One of the best ways to keep your aquarium healthy is never to introduce a new fish without a period of quarantine. Because any new fish have been exposed to many of the risk factors for disease, it's only sensible to keep it well away from the resident population. Even if the new fish looks perfectly healthy, it could be carrying parasites that haven't yet reached full development. Quarantine allows you to observe and perhaps treat new arrivals before introducing them to the healthy community. A safe quarantine period is 3 weeks. After 21 days, you can be fairly certain the new fish won't infect your healthy fish. After 4 weeks, you can be confident the fish is safe to move to the community.

Quarantine/Hospital Tanks

A quarantine, or hospital, tank need not be elaborate. Set up a bare-bottomed tank—appropriately sized to the fish—with a cultured sponge filter, airstone, heater and light. A flowerpot or other non-porous, aquarium-safe object can be used to offer shelter for nervous fish. Be sure the water chemistry and temperature in the new tank are correct before you bring your new fish home or when removing a sick fish from the community. Acclimate the fish to the new water and release it into the quarantine tank. Keep the lights dim for 24 hours to reduce stress.

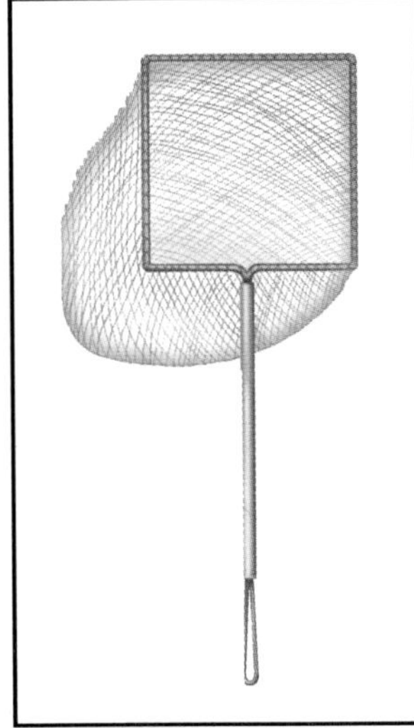

Keep a fishnet on hand that's for use only in the quarantine tank.

Unless there's a life-threatening condition, always allow 24 to 48 hours before beginning any treatment to give the fish time to become acclimated to the new tank.

Keep careful records of when you changed the tank's water, when you noticed your fish becoming ill, when you moved it to the hospital tank and when and what medications you have applied. It's easy to forget which medicine you've used for which symptoms, how much medicine you've used or just when a water change is due unless you write it down. It's also useful to have a record of your successful treatments should you encounter the same problem in the future.

Keep the water in similar condition to that of the main aquarium through testing and water changes, and be sure to keep plenty of conditioned water on hand for water changes. Some treatments require large water changes before adding medications and after treatment.

Always use separate nets, hoses and other equipment for the quarantine/hospital tank.

The Fishy Physical

Examine all your fish every day for clamped fins, frayed fins, open wounds, lesions and unusual skin conditions, such as excessive mucus production, whitish areas, spots, lumps, bumps, protruding eyes or scales, and hemorrhages. Examine the gills to make sure they're beating uniformly. Closed gills or labored breathing is a sign of trouble, possibly resulting from gill flukes, infection or water toxicity. Observe each fish to be sure it's eating and eliminating properly. A trail of white feces from the vent of a fish is a sign of intestinal parasites. Observe the fish's behavior, too. Listlessness, shyness and erratic swimming are all signs of poor health. A fish that faces the rear wall of the tank is silently indicating that it is unwell; it isn't ignoring you in the hope you will go away.

Most fish diseases have their own particular set of symptoms, but some require the use of a microscope to accurately diagnose them.

Injuries

The most common problems that plague cichlids are injuries from tankmates. When a fish is injured, remove it from the community to the hospital tank. If you don't have a hospital tank set up, at least place a divider between the injured fish and the rest of the population. Often, a pair must be separated by a divider when the male is annoying and damaging the female.

Angelfish are susceptible to fin injuries from pugnacious tankmates (Pterophyllum scalare).

Injuries are generally treated with isolation and salt. The isolation gives the fish a chance to gather its resources free from the stress of bullying, and the salt is excellent for increasing the production of slime and healing the skin and fins.

Maintain the fish in the salt bath for as long as 2 weeks or until the wounds are completely healed. A salt bath is also useful for treating external

parasites, gill flukes, some bacterial infections and nitrate poisoning.

To make a salt bath, add 4 ounces of plain salt per 10 gallons of water. Dissolve the salt in a small amount of water before adding it to the tank. At the end of the treatment, remove the salt through normal water changes.

Fungus

Fungus lives in the aquarium, feeding on detritus until conditions are right for it to infect your fish. Injury, disease, poor water quality and chilling all create opportunities for fungus to take hold on your fish.

A fungal infection is particularly troublesome when it develops at the site of a wound. You will undoubtedly see the fungus, which looks like cottony white filaments. You must act quickly if you notice fungus (usually *Saprolegnia* spp.) because it's working its way toward the inside of the fish, secreting toxins into the flesh.

Fungal infections are often treated in a bath with malachite green until signs of the fungus are gone. Malachite green is commercially available and should be used according to the manufacturer's directions.

External Parasites

Ich

Ich, *Ichthyophthirius multifilis,* is a mean parasitic protozoan that produces small white spots on the body and/or gills. Ich is found in fishes all over the world and can cause serious disease. It's often found in fish that have been chilled or stressed by a move. Ich can be present in the aquarium even after treatment because the eggs (cysts) aren't affected by medication, so even after your fishes look well again, they can be re-infested by the newly hatched parasites.

The best therapy for ich requires several steps and 3 weeks before all the parasites are eliminated. Start with a 50 percent water change, including wiping down the glass and vacuuming the gravel. When you replace the water, increase the temperature to about 80° to 90°F. Warm temperatures speed up the life cycle of the parasite, forcing the cysts to hatch earlier than usual and making it possible for the young parasites to be killed by the medication.

There are several medicines that kill off the free-swimming parasites, including the salt therapy mentioned earlier, but ich is most commonly treated with heat and a formalin/malachite green combination, which is available commercially.

Velvet

Hobbyists often confuse velvet with ich. Ich shows up as white spots on the fish, but velvet produces yellowish spots on the fish's body. Velvet, or *Oodinium,* is another external parasite that shows up after a new fish has been introduced or when the fish have been stressed somehow. As with ich, providing warmth helps control this parasite. If you can create a situation in which the parasite's newly hatched young can't find a host fish within 3 weeks, the tank will be clear. Otherwise, raise the tank temperature and treat with copper according to the manufacturer's directions.

Bacterial Infections

Often, bacterial infections are a sign of poor water quality because the bacteria that erode fins and destroy tissues thrive in dirty water. Usually, when a bacterial infection is present, the fish are very weak and lie on the bottom. You may also see loss of appetite and wasting in the fish. Other signs of bacterial infection include ulcers, hemorrhages, protruding scales and pop-eye.

If you suspect a bacterial infection, try a salt bath after a water change, and humanely dispose of any fishes that are obviously dying. Acriflavine is often used for bacterial and protozoan infections.

Good water quality goes far toward preventing the outbreak of bacterial infections. Keep your fish (Heros festivus) *healthy by maintaining your water!*

Intestinal Parasites

Intestinal parasites cause wasting, loss of appetite and generally sick-looking cichlids. A fish with nematodes or flagellates sometimes shows white, trailing feces, and those with tapeworms excrete sections of the worm, which look like a piece of heavy white thread.

Nematodes, flagellates and tapeworms are the most common intestinal parasites of cichlids and can be treated with medicated food or medication applied directly to the water.

One treatment for nematodes, such as capillaria, is piperazine citrate, 0.25 percent, mixed with food and given every day for 5 to 7 days. Fish carrying nematodes often show white slimy feces, and you will probably notice they're facing the back of the tank and looking darker in color.

Hexamita, a condition caused by a flagellate, is associated with hole-in-the-head, scalloped fins and white feces. To treat hexamita, elevate the temperature to 88° to 90°F and add 250 mg. of metronidazole for each 10 gallons of water. Leave the medication in the water for 5 days. If the fish are still showing signs of flagellates, repeat the process in 2 weeks.

Tapeworms are usually discovered when the aquarist sees a section of the worm. To remove them (and several other kinds of parasites), you need to use praziquantel. Crush one 34 mg. tablet into each 10 gallons of water for a 3-day bath.

Bloat

Bloat is often associated with African cichlids, especially *Tropheus* spp. Many aquarists believe it's caused by feeding too much meat to fishes that need a lot of vegetable matter in their diet. Other causes of bloat can be parasitic or bacterial, but to help prevent bloat in cichlids, know the dietary requirements of your fish and follow them.

A fish with bloat has a grossly distended abdominal area, to the point where the scales and even the eyes may stick straight out. Antibiotics have no affect on bloat, but adding adult brine shrimp and vegetables to the diet can help prevent this condition.

A diet that meets your African cichlid's requirements helps keep it from developing bloat (Jewel cichlid with fry, Hemichromis bimaculatus).

Treatments

If you believe you have a sick fish, always start with the least toxic treatment recommended for the disease you suspect. Remember that your fish has the will to live, and given that, it will likely recover. It may be that the infectious agent can be sufficiently reduced with a salt bath or other simple treatment and that the fish's own immune system will recover the power to fight off the disease.

Ideally, you would remove all the fish to a hospital tank for treatment. After 3 weeks, the show tank would be clear of parasites because eggs or cysts would have hatched within this time and without a host fish, they would have died off soon after. However, it's not always possible to move all of your fish to a separate tank, so you might have to be more creative.

First, remove any plants to a separate container with a light source that will keep them healthy for a quarantine period. Plants are sensitive to most medications and often don't survive treatments. Assume that whatever organism is attacking your fish is also attached in some way to the plants, so plan on quarantining them for 3 to 4 weeks.

THE OLD-FASHIONED SALT BATH

The salt bath is the most time-tested cure-all of the fish world. Sometimes called the "progressive saltwater treatment," it's what the hospital tank is most often used for. Simply add 1 teaspoon of table salt (not iodized) for each gallon of water to the hospital tank that houses your fish. Add the same amount of salt that night and twice the next day—again, in the morning and at night. If you don't see any improvements by the third or fourth day, add 1 more teaspoon of salt each day. On the ninth and tenth days, make progressive water changes and check for results.

Before beginning any treatment, you must perform a 50 percent water change with conditioned water. The water change is necessary because many medications won't work if there is a lot of organic waste in the water. Wipe down the inside glass and siphon the gravel well. Clean the filter material.

If you have one available, run a micron-cartridge or diatom filter. These fine-meshed filters capture excess organic matter and reduce the population of parasites and bacteria. After using one of these filters, you may find that the fish begin to recover without further treatment.

If you need to continue with some therapy, remove all carbon from the system before adding medication. The carbon removes some or all of the medicine, so it should be reserved for use after the treatment is finished.

At the end of every treatment, remove the medication from the water. Again, perform a 50 to 100 percent water change with properly conditioned water. Keep activated carbon on hand to draw out residual medications at the end of treatments. You can place the carbon in a mesh bag inside a box filter or small power filter. After 48 hours, the carbon should have effectively cleared the water of chemicals, so you can discard it.

Aquarium Medications

The most frequently used aquarium medications—salt, acriflavine and methylene blue—eliminate many fish diseases. Other common and powerful medications are formalin and malachite green (separately or in combination), copper, metronidazole, praziquantel and piperazine citrate.

Most medications are available at your local pet shop, but you might need to see a veterinarian or visit a livestock feed store for wormers such as praziquantel or piperazine. Aquarium medications should be used with care. Read the packaging to learn which diseases each brand name is meant to treat. Often, commercial medications contain a combination of ingredients that cure a number of conditions commonly found together. Always be sure to follow the package directions precisely because the strengths vary from manufacturer to manufacturer.

Do not mix medications. Although some chemicals can be safely combined, others are toxic in combination, and it's difficult to know just what the outcome will be. Finally, always keep all aquarium medications out of the reach of children!

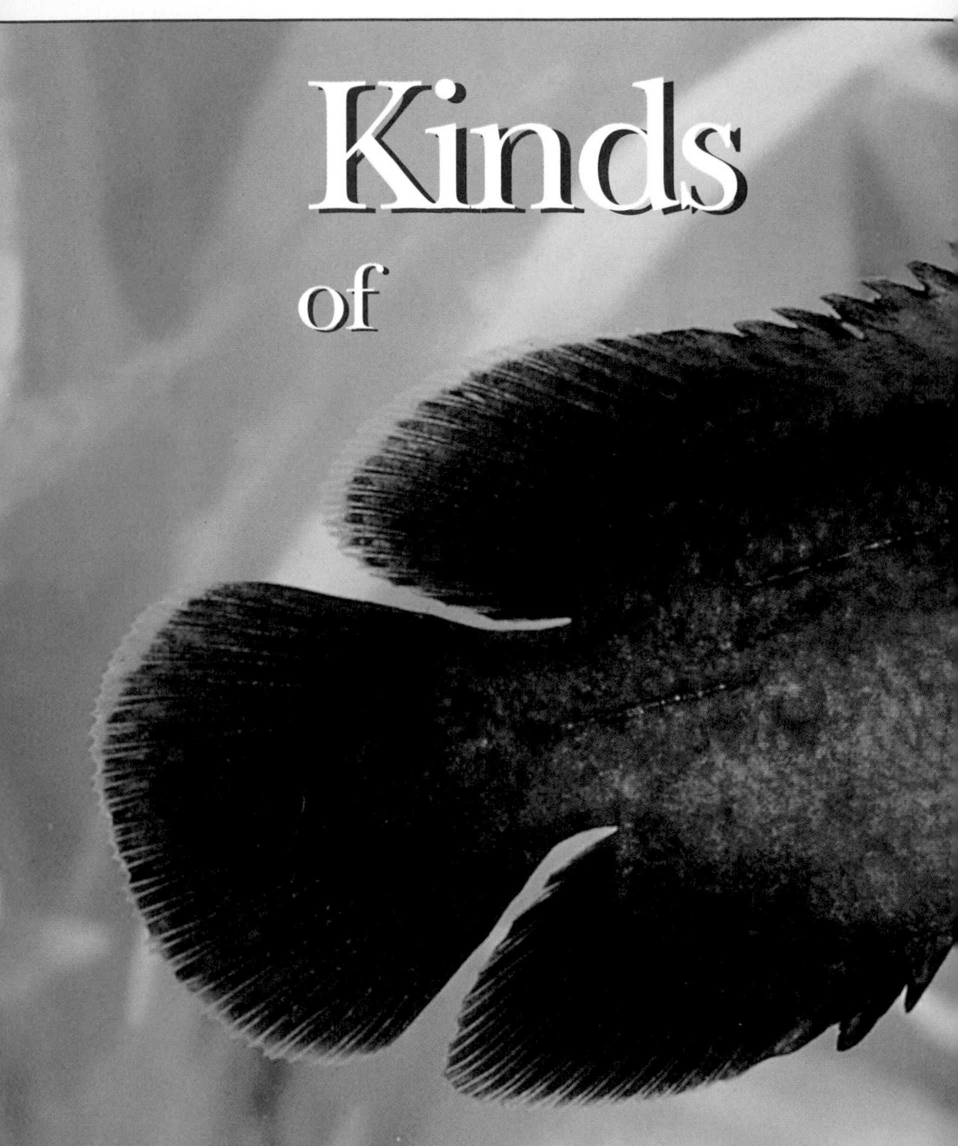
Kinds
of

part three

Cichlids

chapter 8

Dwarf Cichlids

Dwarf cichlids are dainty, beautifully shaped and often vividly colored. They look and behave their best in the kind of beautifully planted and decorated tank that makes any aquarist's heart beat faster. Dwarf cichlids are not plant terminators, so plant away!

Dwarf cichlids include species from Africa and the Americas, but they have certain important features in common. All dwarf cichlids are less than 4 inches long. A pair or a trio of one male and two females can be comfortably housed in a 10- or 15-gallon aquarium, but larger groups can be kept in bigger tanks and even in community tanks with peaceful schools of tetras and various types of catfish. These fish spend most of their time at the lower levels of the water column, so floor space is much more important for them than tank height.

Dwarf cichlids are generally the most peaceful of cichlids, but naturally get a bit belligerent at spawning time or when they are guarding eggs or young.

Housing for Dwarf Cichlids

For dwarf cichlids, think of shadowy, safe places where the fish could hide from predators if they were in the wild. Dwarf cichlids like plenty of plants, driftwood, small rockwork structures, caves made from halved clay flowerpots and as many small niches as you can arrange.

Use fine-grained sand or very fine gravel, preferably of a natural or dark color. For the shell dwellers, such as *Lamprologus ornatipinnis,* an assortment of snail shells and fine sand are necessary ingredients of good fish husbandry.

Because these fish enjoy plants in the aquarium, it's important to include them in their environment. The challenge is to provide enough light to keep the plants healthy without stressing the fish; dwarf cichlids generally avoid bright light. You can overcome this problem, however, by using low-light plants, such as Java Fern *(Microsorium pteropus)* and Java Moss *(Vesicularia dubyana)* near the bottom of the tank and light-loving floating plants, such as *Riccia fluitans,* at the waterline. As the plants "fill in," the fish will feel more secure, and you will see them more frequently.

The water chemistry where the South American dwarf cichlids are found varies between the dry and the rainy season and from place to place. The water is usually a bit harder and more alkaline in the dry season, but it's preferable to keep them in the soft, acidic water which is the norm. West African dwarf cichlids appreciate the same kind of tank setup, perhaps with some slight changes in water chemistry.

Tanganyikan dwarf cichlids, on the other hand, must be kept like their larger African cousins in the hard, alkaline conditions of the rift lake. Dwarf cichlids do require careful attention to water quality because they

are famously sensitive to elevated ammonia, nitrite and nitrate levels in the water.

The best water temperature for most dwarf cichlids is usually between 79° and 82°F. Because dwarf cichlids are generally tropical species, it's very important that they do not get chilled, so keep an eye on the thermometer.

Feeding dwarf cichlids is not difficult. They are generally omnivorous, taking a wide variety of live and prepared foods, with a special fondness for live brine shrimp and small worms. To bring them into peak condition, give them lots of live and frozen foods.

"Apistos," like many dwarf cichlids, are cave spawners (Apistogramma panduro).

South American Dwarf Cichlids

South American waters are home to many cichlids, both the standard size and the dwarfs. Dwarf cichlids live in small pools near the banks and enjoy shallow water with plenty of hiding places.

Genus *Apistogramma*

The genus *Apistogramma* contains around 70 species, with 50 described species and about another 20 waiting for scientific evaluation.

These fish are excellent aquarium residents, known for peacefulness, attractive coloration and ease of care.

They are shy and will show their best only if given many hiding places. Be sure to give them a number of safe places to scoot off to if they get scared.

There are distinct differences between males and females. Like many dwarf cichlids, "Apistos" are cave spawners that lay their eggs inside caves (like a halved flowerpot). If the male is ready to spawn and the female isn't, he harasses her to the point of death. Assuming that successful breeding does take place, the female takes care of the eggs and the fry, and the male protects the breeding site. If their quarters are cramped, the female savages the male when she is guarding the eggs. He's evicted from the area and, with no place to escape, may even be killed. In some fish, the male helps the female take care of the fry after they are free-swimming.

Agassiz' Dwarf Cichlid

Apistogramma agassizii, the Agassiz' Dwarf Cichlid, is among the most popular of the dwarf cichlids. The males, which are much more colorful than the females, are approximately $3^1/_2$ inches long, but the females reach only 2 inches. The fins are rounded in the females. There are several color varieties: blue-white, yellow and red.

The Agassiz' Dwarf Cichlid is available in several color varieties: blue-white, yellow and red.

The Agassiz' Dwarf Cichlid requires soft, acidic water with a pH of 5.0 to 6.0. Give this fish a large tank with

plenty of floor space. Dark, fine gravel brings out the best colors in the fish. Give them plenty of plants, caves, rocks and driftwood.

Among Borelli's Dwarf Cichlids, females establish the territories in the tank.

Borelli's Dwarf Cichlid

Apistogramma borellii, Borelli's Dwarf Cichlid, is a territorial fish during breeding season but is otherwise a peaceful cichlid. Several females should be housed with a single male. The male hovers in the upper water column watching the females who have established territories in caves below, an unusual habit in cichlids. The Borelli's Dwarf Cichlid lives harmoniously in a mature, but understocked, peaceful aquarium.

Three-Striped Dwarf Cichlid

Apistogramma trifasciata, the Three-Striped Dwarf Cichlid, is also commonly known as the Blue Apisto. This fish is territorial and polygamous. It needs a large tank for one male and several females, and each female needs a cave of her own. The female's maternal instincts are exceptionally strong, to the point of stealing fry from other females and even adopting live foods as part of the family.

GENUS *Dicrossus*

Checkerboard Lyretail

Dicrossus filamentosus, the Checkerboard Lyretail, is a popular member of the *Dicrossus* genus. With its lyretail and vivid colors, this cichlid could easily be mistaken for a killifish. It shows a good deal of variation in color and pattern based on its feelings. When Checkerboard Lyretails are stressed, like most cichlids, they appear washed out and quite plain, but when they are properly kept or in breeding dress, they are spectacular. They are not overly shy and can be kept with other peaceful fishes in a small tank with soft, acidic water with a pH of 5.0. They do best in a warm tank kept at about 82°F.

It's easy to see how the Checkerboard Lyretail got its name!

Genus *Laetacara*

Species in the *Laetacara* genus, including the Curviceps and Dorsigera, are quite feisty for dwarf cichlids and have healthy appetites. They do not tolerate poor water quality well at all, so be sure not to miss water changes. Again, keep them in soft, acidic, warm water with plenty of plants. They may eat some of the plants, but they won't do much damage to them.

You can spot a Curviceps by the black line running from its eye to its tail.

Curviceps

Aequidens curviceps, the Curviceps, is a 3-inch fish with a chunky blue-spangled body and a distinct black line from the eye to the tail. The water should be soft to medium-hard with a pH of 6.0 to 6.8.

Regular water changes are critical for this species because they are extremely sensitive to nitrites.

GENUS *Microgeophagus*

Ram

The Ram, *Microgeophagus ramirezi,* is without a doubt the best-known and most popular of all the dwarf cichlids. Rams are a relatively good choice for mixed community tanks. There are several types currently available on the market, including the German Blue Ram, which (not surprisingly) shows a great deal more blue than wild fish, and the Golden Ram, which is bright yellow. These fish must be kept properly. Soft, acidic water and a heavily planted tank are necessary, or they will never be seen.

For a cichlid, Rams get along rather well in a community tank.

GENUS *Nannacara*

Golden Dwarf Cichlids

Nannacara anomala, the Golden Dwarf Cichlid, is very peaceful and shy. They are slightly more liberal about water chemistry than other dwarf cichlids, as long as the pH is kept at or below neutral. The female loses her shyness when she has eggs or fry to defend, so it might be wise to remove the male to a safe tank at this time.

Males are more brightly colored and larger than females.

African Dwarf Cichlids

African dwarf cichlids, like those from South America, can be kept in small, well-planted and well-furnished tanks. Water conditions are variable, depending on where the fish originates, but many of the riverine African dwarf cichlids require soft, acidic water, as do most of the South American species.

Golden Dwarf Cichlids are known for their shyness.

Genus *Eretemodus*

Striped Goby Cichlid

The Striped Goby Cichlid, *eretemodus cyanostictus,*is a funny little fish with an overhanging snout. It's difficult to keep and hard to breed because of its stringent requirements for water quality. Give this native of Lake Tanganyika a rock-filled tank with the correct pH (from 8.5 to 9.0) and appropriate hardness (dH of 12° to 15°).

A Jewel Cichlid shows off its elaborate coloration (Hemichromis bimaculatus).

The Striped Goby Cichlid may be small at 3 inches, but it's quite territorial and unfriendly toward members of its own species. As breeding adults, they are monogamous, with both parents caring for the young.

Genus *Hemichromis*

The Jewel Cichlids, *Hemichromis* spp., are as feisty as they are beautiful. These small fish are especially brilliant during breeding season, when their bright red color with its iridescent quality is stunning. They are very aggressive, even between the male and female, so they can be a bit

difficult to keep. The water should be in the neutral range with a temperature of about 75°F.

The bright red color of this Jewel Cichlid indicates its breeding season (Hemichromis lifalili).

GENUS *Julidochromis*

The Julie, *Julidochromis dickfeldi,* is known by some as the Brown Julie. This is a petite cichlid, growing to only 3 inches long. Other *Julidochromis* species vary in size, with *J. regani* reaching up to 12 inches. These fish need many rocky caves, especially because they're extremely territorial and hard on members of their own kind. They do accept all kinds of foods and are especially fond of brine shrimp.

GENUS NEOLAMPROLOGUS

Neolamprologus is a large genus with many species that hails from Lake Tanganyika. *N. brevis* is a small fish that is 2 1/2 or 3 inches long; the females are even smaller. This is a shell-dweller that requires some snail shells for its comfort. A substrate of fine sand completes the picture.

Fairy Cichlid

The Fairy Cichlid, *N. brichardi,* is probably the most beautiful member of this genus. It has a modest length of just under 4 inches and an elegant body shape and fins. A group of these fish can be kept well in a small tank with many rocks and stones. They don't molest plants, so don't hesitate to include them in this fish's tank.

Lemon Cichlid

N. leleupi, the Lemon Cichlid, is exquisite with its bright yellow coloration. It's a fish that needs a fine, sandy bottom and very good water quality. Plenty of live foods, such as brine shrimp, keep this fish happy and healthy.

Lemon Cichlids thrive on live foods.

Genus *Pelvicachromis*

Kribensis

The Kribensis is a peace-loving fish that's often kept in community tanks.

Kribensis, *Pelvicachromis pulcher,* can also be found under the common name Purple Cichlid. Kribensis are probably the best known of the African dwarf cichlids and are peaceful, timid cichlids. They can even be kept in community tanks as long as they aren't harassed by their tankmates. In their natural habitat, the pH is quite low, around 5.0, and the water is very, very soft. If your Kribensis have been tank-raised, they might not need such drastic water conditions, but the water must be kept very clean.

Asian Dwarf Cichlids

It's unusual for hobbyists to find dwarf cichlids from Asia, but you will certainly want to consider them for your aquarium.

Orange Chromide enjoy a well-planted tank.

> **A RARE BEAUTY**
>
> The genus *Nanochromis* contains many species of varying availability. One of the most beautiful, Dimidiatus *(Nanochromis dimidiatus)*, is a bit hard to find but well worth keeping. They can be aggressive at breeding time, especially if they are kept in a small tank. The pair sometimes fight after spawning, so be prepared to remove the submissive fish, whether it's male or female, and be sure there are plenty of hiding places. Dimidiatus should be kept in soft, acidic water.

Genus *Etroplus*

Orange Chromide

The Orange Chromide, *Etroplus maculatus,* is a native of India and Sri Lanka. This 3-inch cichlid favors a slightly brackish tank with the addition of about 1 teaspoon of salt to a gallon of water. The Orange Chromide is peaceful but should not be kept with smaller fishes that it will certainly eat. It prefers live and frozen foods. Give this lovely yellow and black fish a planted tank with a sandy bottom for sifting and a few flat rocks, and it will do very well.

chapter 9

Old World Cichlids

The "Old World" cichlids include species from Africa and points east, such as India. The dwarf cichlids from African waters are discussed in chapter 8, "Dwarf Cichlids."

The most popular and plentiful of the Old World cichlids are those from the rift lakes of Malawi and Tanganyika. Of these, the group known as *mbuna* are the most familiar to the hobbyist.

What Are Mbuna?

Mbuna—often called Malawis—are not the only cichlids found in Lake Malawi, but they are a special, exceptionally beautiful group of

rock-dwelling fishes. Lake Malawi, a "rift lake" (bounded by the countries of Malawi, Tanzania and Mozambique), is one of a few ancient bodies of water, including Lakes Tanganyika and Victoria, that were formed by violent eruptions that cracked the surface of the earth. Lake Malawi is full of cichlids, perhaps more different kinds than any other lake in the world.

Mbuna, which means "rock fish" in the local language, has no scientific meaning at all. There are 10 genera of mbuna: *Pseudotropheus, Melanochromis, Petrotilapia, Labidochromis, Cynotilapia, Labeotropheus, Gephyrochromis, Iodotropheus, Genyochromis* and *Cyathochromis. Aulonocara* is a member of another group, the non-mbuna haplochromines. Because of the similar habits of *Aulonocara* (and perhaps also because they are so beautiful), these rock-dwelling species have been assigned a place of honor among the mbuna.

Identifying the many species of mbuna is a challenge best left to scientists. Common names and the names used by individual sellers for these fishes have made them an identification nightmare, even at the expert level. In fact, many of the fish discussed here and in the following chapter have no common name. Accordingly, some species are referred to only by their scientific name.

Physical Characteristics

Mbuna are not particularly large for cichlids; very few of them grow to be more than 8 inches long. While this is a respectable size in the aquarium, it's not a big fish overall. Many times, these fish grow larger in the aquarium than they do in the wild.

They are all, without exception, brightly colored and beautifully proportioned. Because mbuna are grazers or pickers, they are not built for rapid swimming. Although they are quite capable of short bursts of speed, they are usually quite sedate—sizing up the situation for possible danger or a feeding opportunity. They move almost stiffly between their chosen spot and any other destination, back and forth and up and down with almost robot-like movements. Because they live among the rocks, they tend to be elongated and slender to facilitate their passage through tight crevices.

Mbuna tend to have long, slender bodies that enhance their ability to move through their rock-filled environment (Pseudotropheus socolofi).

Mbuna Behavior

I wish I could say that good behavior was common in mbuna, but they tend to be rather unsocial creatures, even quite nasty sometimes. Because of their good looks, no doubt, aquarists have worked to develop ways to keep them successfully with minimal bloodshed.

In territorial mbuna species, the males are extremely so. The best accommodation is to keep only one male in an aquarium with several (three or even more) females to keep him well diverted. If you want to have more than one species in the same aquarium, choose a species that's very different in appearance. This trick may reduce aggression between the males. The territoriality of male mbuna reflects the fact that all spawning takes place in his territory, and he must defend the spawning site from intruders. The female is mildly territorial when in the male's territory, which is only right because she's merely visiting.

You will often see jaw-locking between mbuna, and although it looks nasty, it's not the worst form of

fighting in these fish. They have very tough mouths that aren't easily damaged. It is more serious when a fish approaches another at a right angle and bites the other's flank. Because mbuna are armed with formidable teeth, such attacks can inflict terrible damage. They chew the tails and fins off their rivals, too. If the victim assumes the correct submissive posture, the attack is called off, but that doesn't usually happen.

Keeping Mbuna

Lake Malawi cichlids are creatures of habit. They like to eat the same food, and they like to stay in the same place in the aquarium, so make sure you take these habits into consideration when creating the perfect aquarium for mbuna. There's no benefit to depriving them of the furnishings that allow them to live most fully, and this includes breeding and fry care.

> **ONE WAY TO KEEP THE PEACE**
>
> Some hobbyists keep aggression in check by stocking only males in the tank. Males are usually more colorful than females, and with no female fish around, there's little reason to squabble. The trick is to identify male fish; most fish are sold as juveniles that don't yet have their full coloration.

Lake Malawi is very rocky, and these rocks are home to mbuna and an essential feature for their well-being. The rocks in the lake give the fish a personal territory, spawning areas, protection and a site for food colonies. Is it any wonder that mbuna seldom care to leave their chosen places and defend the site so ferociously? Their protective nature can be the start of fierce territorial battles that ultimately leave only one winner: the owner of the rock! The losers of these battles aren't hard to identify: They are usually hanging out near a top corner of the aquarium with ripped fins, missing scales, washed-out color and a very depressed demeanor.

You should never permit this kind of interaction in the aquarium, and there are ways to contain the aggressive tendencies of mbuna (and many, many other species of cichlids, too). Just what triggers a clash of the Titans in your mbuna aquarium? By examining how their societies operate below the surface of the lake, you gain an understanding of how the aquarium should be set up.

Fish fights are destructive, so they definitely shouldn't be encouraged. I am always struck by the number of people who keep large, predatory fishes in a community environment, and I wish they would find another hobby. Most genuine hobbyists lose fish in error, not because of a perverse desire to pit fish against fish in a continuous battle. There is a fine balance struck between the fish in a community tank. It involves some knowledge of the behavior of fishes, acute observational skills and, of course, the fishes themselves. When you know that two males of the same species behave as mortal enemies, why try to force them to live together? Use the instinctive behavior of the fish to create a harmonious balance in the aquarium.

When setting up your dream mbuna aquarium, arrange the rockwork so that the male's territory is visible to you in its entirety. You will see how the females are free to roam in the water column, how the male lures them into his territory and how the eggs are laid and then picked up to be carried in the female's mouth until they hatch and are ready to swim free. Fascinating!

WHAT'S A MOUTHBROODER?

Mouthbrooders are fish that actually carry their eggs in their mouths. As soon as the eggs are laid, one parent immediately places them in its mouth; eventually, the eggs hatch, and the fry venture out. While the eggs are incubating, the adult fish accepts no food. Interestingly, the fry often attempt to re-enter the parent's mouth, looking as though they're trying to be eaten.

Aquarium Techniques

Mbuna are found in clear, alkaline waters in and around rocks of different shapes and sizes. This is the type of habitat you want to re-create for them in the aquarium. The water should be hard, around 10° to 15°dH. The pH should be around 8.0.

The water temperature at the shorelines where mbuna are found averages around 78°F. It's best to keep the temperature steady, so don't permit wide fluctuations either up or down. High temperatures speed up the metabolism of the fishes and cause early death (or even sudden death if the temperature is too high). Although a sudden rise in temperature is more easily tolerated than a sudden drop of the same degree, as water heats up it becomes less able to carry oxygen. In a heavily stocked aquarium, this might be fatal to the fishes. As the temperature rises, so does the activity level of the fishes. This could be trouble in a tank that's at capacity already, particularly in the high pH conditions under which you keep mbuna. The high pH, high ammonia, high temperature and low oxygen are responsible for most of the sudden die-offs that perplex fish-keepers.

As a rule, mbuna prefer to stay near the bottom of the tank (Zebra Cichlid).

Mbuna are inclined to stay near the bottom of the tank and surface only reluctantly for special treats. This is a good reason to give them rectangular tanks with a lot of floor space.

For mbuna, you can use a dark or naturally colored gravel or sand in combination with crushed coral. The coral contains calcium carbonate, which helps stabilize the water's pH level. The best substrate is about 3 inches of natural-colored pebbles mixed 50-50 with the coral. The pebbles should be rounded and even in size. Your mbuna will delight in taking mouthfuls and moving the gravel around and piling it up into little hills. Darker colors tend to make the fish look and feel better.

GENUS *Aulonocara*

The genus *Aulonocara* contains many attractive and desirable fishes, often called Peacock Cichlids.

Aulonocara benefit from a sandy substrate. Some species like to hover motionless above the sand and then dive head-first into the sand to snap up tiny invertebrates. In the aquarium, however, they seldom have the opportunity to feed in this manner. They are eager eaters and take flake foods with enthusiasm.

These are the most peaceful of the Malawi cichlids, but territorial males in breeding coloration should be respected. Make sure you protect the *Aulonocara* from more aggressive mbuna. They are usually bred in species tanks with one male and three females in a tank of about 20 gallons. When the male is defending his territory, he builds a nest in the sand.

African Peacock

Aulonocara nyassae, the African Peacock, is about as lovely a fish as you would want to see, with the male showing a white or light blue edge on the dorsal fin and a deep-blue body with iridescent highlights. The female is plainer, but an attractive fish, nonetheless. This is a territorial but relatively peaceful species that grows to about 6 inches long.

Peacock Cichlids like to dive into the sand in search of food but will be happy with commercial food in the aquarium (Aulonocara jacobfreibergi).

Genus *Iodotropheus*

Members of the *Iodotropheus* genus, such as the Rusty Cichlid and Grant's Malawi Cichlid, are small, non-territorial mbuna usually found in pairs or small groups. They are reddish-brown fish with a purple-violet cast to each scale. Some species are known to indulge in in-fighting, but on the whole are less aggressive than many of the other mbuna species. They are commonly available and relatively inexpensive.

GENUS *Labeotropheus*

Fuelleborn's Cichlid and the Red-Topped Trewavasae are members of the genus *Labeotropheus.* These fishes are most easily identified by their overhanging snouts, rather than by their color. There are several lovely color-morphs within the *Labeotropheus* genus, including an albino (the male is pale blue, and the female is yellow, both with red eyes), a predominantly orange morph and one with a red dorsal (a red top).

A well-developed snout is typical of the Red-Topped Trewavasae.

The males constantly pursue the females, so it is best to keep several females to each male. Two males can be kept only in very large tanks because of their aggressive behavior.

GENUS *Labidochromis*

Labidochromis is a large genus with many species, but they are physically the smallest of the mbuna. *Labidochromis caeruleus* is one of the most popular of the Malawi cichlids with its bright yellow body and blue, almost black, dorsal fin.

The males defend their territories vigorously in the aquarium. A community of these fishes, including more than one male, can be kept successfully if there are enough rocky territories. The dominant male remains in high color most of the time. When designing your rockwork, each territory should be somewhat self-contained, with no direct line of vision to the other territories in the tank. If the fishes cannot readily see each other from their own territories, they don't usually go looking for trouble.

GENUS *Melanochromis*

Melanochromis auratus, the Malawi Golden Cichlid, also commonly known as Auratus, and the other commonly available species—*M. chipokae, M. exasperatus, M. johanni* and *M. vermivorus*—differ from most mbuna by having horizontal, rather than vertical, stripes, and most attractive ones, too. Also interesting is the reversal of pigmentation patterns in males and females (the male is dark where the female is light, and vice versa) of some of the species. They are slender, elongate fishes with wide mouths and slightly thickened lips.

These fishes are usually only mildly territorial in the lake, and the many species are colorful and excellent in the aquarium. Nonetheless, the crowded conditions of life in the aquarium do not bring out their best behavior. Any mbuna should be considered aggressive and territorial in an aquarium until you observe that its behavior is otherwise. As it happens, members of the genus *Melanochromis* are ferocious in protecting their breeding site, so large aquariums with tankmates of other hardy species are required.

Members of the Melanochromis *genus, such as the Malawi Golden Cichlid, have unusual horizontal stripes.*

GENUS *Pseudotropheus*

The *Pseudotropheus* genus contains many species, including the best-known of all the mbuna, the Zebra Cichlid, also known as the Nyassa Blue Cichlid, *Pseudotropheus zebra.* This is the fish that has enchanted so many of the people who have become involved with African cichlids. It's readily available and easy to breed.

P. acei

P. acei is a gorgeous fish with a black body, blue face and bright yellow on the tail and dorsal. The female is similar to the male, but more subdued in color.

P. aurora

P. aurora is a blue fish splashed with yellow-gold beneath the body and on the fins. The female is solid pale yellow. It's a lovely fish to look at but has a bad reputation for aggression.

The beauty of P. aurora is only skin-deep—this is a nasty fish!

Slender Mbuna

P. elongatus, the Slender Mbuna, is an elongated fish, easily identified by its long, slender body. Both sexes are blue with broad, dark, vertical bands, but the males are a much deeper blue with a dark head. There are many complaints about the aggressiveness of this fish, but it should be noted that captive-bred specimens are generally less boisterous than their wild-caught cousins.

P. greshakei

P. greshakei is one of the "red tops," fish that sport red dorsal fins and some red on the tail, too, which is a very desirable characteristic.

P. lanisticola

P. lanisticola lives in empty snail shells. As the fish grows, it must look for larger and larger shells. They are quite nasty, so give them many shells and other holes to help maintain the peace. These fish are generally either bluish or yellowish; the bluish one is the breeding male.

P. livingstoni

P. livingstoni lives mainly in sandy areas and uses snail shells as its refuge and spawning area. When keeping this species, some large, empty apple snail or escargot shells make it feel right at home.

P. lombardoi

P. lombardoi females and juveniles are a bluish color with black barring. The adult males take on a striking golden color with black barring. The males are very aggressive within their own species but generally leave other species alone.

Keep adult males of the P. lombardoi species separated—consider only one per tank.

Golden Tropheops

P. tropheops, commonly called Golden Tropheops, has many varieties based on beautiful color forms and their location within the lake. *Tropheops* was one of the first mbuna known to science. They are recognized by the profile of their snouts, which have a steep downward slope.

Zebra Cichlid

Varieties of the Zebra Cichlid are commonly found in aquariums, are very easy to keep and make an excellent

beginner's fish. If not given its own space, a Zebra can be quite quarrelsome, so be sure not to crowd these fish.

In the wild, Zebra males defend territories centered on a cave where they spawn or take refuge. Females, youngsters and sub-dominant males are social and travel together in schools.

Because Zebra Cichlids are less challenging than many other fishes, they make a great pet for the new hobbyist.

Lake Tanganyika Cichlids

Lake Tanganyika is the home of many brilliantly colored, interesting cichlids. The water of Lake Tanganyika is harder and more alkaline than Lake Malawi. The pH is 8.6 to 9.5 with a total hardness of 11° to 17° dH.

Tanganyikan Cichlid Aquariums

The setup of the Tanganyikan cichlid aquarium is essentially the same as for the Malawi aquarium, except for the differences in water chemistry and increased temperature. Tanganyikans are very sensitive to dissolved metabolic wastes, particularly nitrite. They are difficult to keep in captivity, especially if they're crowded, since nitrite would increase rapidly in a crowded tank. They are intolerant of acidic water, too; a pH level of 7.5 to 8.5 is acceptable. Use a Tanganyika salt mix to buffer the water with crushed oyster shell in the substrate to help prevent lowering the pH. Temperatures may be kept between 78° and 82°F. Bear in mind that these fish do not tolerate swings in water temperature. Stability is the key issue in all things for Tanganyikan cichlids.

Some Tanganyikans dig pits for spawning, but otherwise, they are not serious diggers. Although there are few plants in Lake Tanganyika, you can use low plants in their aquarium, especially *Anubias*. Do not use driftwood for fish that require high pH water; it tends to soften and acidify the water.

Feeding Tanganyikan Cichlids

Do not feed tubifex worms or frozen brine shrimp to these fishes because these foods can lead to internal bacterial infections. Flake and pelleted vegetable foods are good, as are fresh vegetables. They enjoy algaed rocks, too.

Genus *Cyphotilapia*

You can identify an adult male Frontosa Cichlid by its large cranial hump.

Frontosa Cichlid

Cyphotilapia frontosa, the Frontosa Cichlid, is a large fish—but a timid and peaceful one—that occasionally reaches 12 inches long. It's difficult to distinguish the males from females, but older males tend to develop a pronounced hump on the forehead. One male should have several females in the tank with him, and the tank should have rockwork to offer privacy and safety for females. Frontosas can be kept with other peaceful Tanganyikan cichlids.

Because these are large fish, they have large appetites and need plenty of meaty foods, including live fishes from time to time.

GENUS *Cyprichromis*

Cyprichromis species are peaceful, schooling fish, about 5 inches long, that are always kept in groups of at least six fishes. They require a large tank because they're active swimmers, but they don't dig or destroy plants. They make good community tank fishes as long as their tankmates are not so large as to view them as food. Be sure to cover the tank because the females jump during courtship.

GENUS *Julidochromis*

Members of the *Julidochromis* genus—*J. dickfeldi* (Brown Julie), *J. ornatus, J. regani* and *J. transcriptus* (Black and White Julie)—are ideal aquarium fishes except that they do get jealous at spawning time. There are no obvious differences in males and females. "Julies" may be kept in small aquariums of about 20 gallons. These fishes are cave-spawners that appreciate a sandy bottom and rockwork. Julies feed on algae and small crustaceans but will take prepared foods. Daphnia and mosquito larvae are favorites.

Julies come in a wide range of sizes; the J. marlieri *grows to 6 inches long.*

Julies are variable in size. Some, such as *dickfeldi* and *transcriptus,* grow to about 3 inches long and fall within the category of dwarf cichlids. On the other hand, *marlieri* and *regani* can be quite large, up to 6 and 12 inches long, respectively.

GENUS *Tropheus*

Tropheus moori

Tropheus moori is probably the best-known of the Tanganyikan cichlids, even though there are other, more colorful members of the genus.

Mooris are not large fish, reaching about 5 inches long, but because they are aggressive with their own kind, they do need a large aquarium. One male should be given a "harem" of at least six females; however, if they are to be kept with other species of the same genus or other hardy Tanganyikan fishes, one or two females per male is enough.

Mooris feel their best if fed a diet high in vegetables.

Be careful when you're feeding Mooris. Make sure they get enough vegetable matter in their diet, and avoid tubifex worms, blackworms and bloodworms. Earthworms and beef heart are fine, as long as you include vegetables in the diet.

West African Cichlids

There are plenty of cichlids in the lakes of Africa, but West African cichlids are likely to be found in streams and rivers in rainforests and savannahs with the usual acidic, soft water. Many of the West African cichlids are dwarfs (see chapter 8, "Dwarf Cichlids"), but there are a few large West African cichlids that deserve mention.

GENUS *Chromidotilapia*

Chromidotilapia batesii

Chromidotilapia batesii is a mouthbrooder with an unusual parenting style. Known as a *larvophile mouthbrooder,* the female collects the hatched fry in her mouth and holds them there until they are able to be free-swimming. The eggs themselves are laid on the

ceiling of a cave where they incubate under the watchful eyes of their parents. This fish needs plenty of plants, caves and soft, acidic water.

Gunther's Mouthbrooder

Chromidotilapia guntheri, Gunther's Mouthbrooder, is a native of coastal rivers and lagoons. On occasion, this fish is found in hard, alkaline water, even brackish water, but it also resides in rainforests. It's a shy fish that should have plenty of plants and caves. It grows to about 6 inches long, so you need a good-sized tank for it.

Gunther's Mouthbrooder appreciates a tank filled with plants and caves to hide in.

GENUS *Teleogramma*

Teleogramma brichardi

Teleogramma brichardi is a visually interesting character; essentially, it's a deep bluish gray with a white band on the long dorsal fin and the top of the tail. This slim fish that grows to 5 inches long, is quite territorial, so it needs a lot of room in a rocky planted tank. This fish is native to the Zaire River, where the water moves rapidly and has a neutral to slightly acidic pH. Keep *T. brichardi* in a long, low tank with good aeration, and feed it on live, frozen and prepared foods.

chapter 10

New World Cichlids

The Americas are rich in cichlids that you can keep in the home aquarium. South America, especially the Amazon region, is a hothouse for such diverse and interesting fishes as the Oscar, the angelfish, and the discus. Central America is the home of other exciting fish, including many of the "tank busters," such as the Jack Dempsey.

Aquariums for South American Cichlids

Most literature on keeping arrangements for the majority of the South American species suggests using rocks and driftwood and

warm, soft, acidic water. Although cichlids are generally forgiving of less-than-perfect water chemistry, those coming from the Amazon area in particular need careful attention to proper water chemistry and quality.

These fishes do not tolerate chilling. Depending on the species, keep the water between 76° and 82°F. Cold water often leads to disease or early death in these tropical fishes.

Cleanliness is also important in keeping South American cichlids; they are intolerant of neglect. Some of these fishes are relatively large and big eaters, so make sure you supply ample and efficient filtration. Because the typical tank for South American cichlids is kept quite warm, it's advisable to add extra aeration in the form of an air pump and airstone. Warm water holds less oxygen than cooler water, and low oxygen in the water is very hard on most cichlids.

If your tap water is hard and alkaline, maybe you should consider keeping African cichlids or some of the Central American fishes that are comfortable in this type of water. Softening water can become an all-consuming passion for those people with hard water who want to keep fish such as discus. In contrast, raising the hardness and alkalinity of water and lowering the pH is quite simple.

Popular South American Species

Genus *Acarichthys*

Heckel's Acara

Acarichthys heckelii, Heckel's Acara, is an 8-inch fish with long trailers on the fins and blue spots evenly distributed over a brownish-gold body. The fins are quite spectacular. This fish is undemanding with respect to water chemistry and food choices. Unfortunately, it can be a bit hostile. If you're keeping it in a mixed-cichlid community tank, be sure its tank-mates are of equal power and size.

Heckel's Acara is a relatively low-maintenance fish.

Genus *Aequidens*

Blue Acara

Aequidens pulcher, the Blue Acara, hails from Northwestern South America and Trinidad. It's a pretty blue-spangled fish that grows to about 6 to 8 inches long. The Blue Acara is content in water of a neutral nature. This fish eats most aquarium foods but does show a preference for live brine shrimp.

A diet of brine shrimp helps spur the growth of the fry of Green Terrors.

Although the Blue Acara can be feisty at times, if it's given plenty of food and cover, it gets along with other non-aggressive tankmates.

Green Terror

Aequidens rivulatus, the Green Terror, from Eastern Ecuador, is well named, as any 12-inch omnivorous cichlid is likely to throw its weight around. However, it's a glamorous fish well worth keeping. The males sport a cranial hump on the forehead, lots of green iridescence and a snazzy red border on the tail and dorsal fins. If you have the space, consider a big tank with other large, like-minded cichlids.

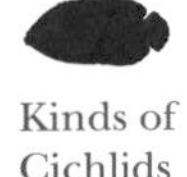

GENUS *Astronotus*

Astronotus ocellatus, the Oscar, is a true pet fish and perhaps the first cichlid most people encounter. The Oscar is found in a wide range, from Venezuela to the Amazon Basin and Paraguay—and the fresh waterways of Florida, thanks to releases by aquarists and escapes from fish farms. In fact, in Florida and other areas they have colonized, Oscars are considered good sport for anglers.

There are several types of Oscars: Red, Albino, Tiger and wild. There's even a long-finned type of Oscar. One distinctive feature of the Oscar is the red "eye spot" at the base of the tail. The Oscar can reach a length of 12 inches at maturity, so it requires a large tank. This is a big fish for all but the largest aquariums and requires at least a 50-gallon tank at maturity.

Oscars have big appetites, so they're messy. If you are planning to keep an Oscar, make sure you have a good filtration system and you change the water regularly.

Remember when purchasing juvenile Oscars that they grow to 1 foot in length; have your aquarium set up to accommodate a large fish (Red Oscar).

Usually, the Oscars in shops are very young, no more than 2 or 3 inches long. Beware! These small babies grow quickly and devour smaller tankmates. Although the Oscar is not overly aggressive toward suitable tankmates, it consumes smaller fish without blinking an eye.

Genus *Biotodoma*

Cupid Cichlid

Biotodoma cupido, the Cupid Cichlid, is a beautiful 6-inch fish with iridescent blue markings on the face and a golden body with hints of orange. This delicate fish requires a warm, acidic tank. Give it plenty of hiding places in the form of plants and driftwood.

Genus *Crenicichla*

Crenicichla regani—also called the Dwarf Pike—at 6 inches long is the smallest of this South American genus. Other pikes, like *C. saxatilis,* the Spangled Pike, grow to 12 inches.

Lots of plants and driftwood give the Cupid Cichlid a sense of security.

Keep pikes in large aquariums with larger dither fish, ample hiding places and a South American habitat of peaty soft water and plants. Use as many live and frozen foods as possible while working pellets into the diet.

Almost all pike cichlids have an unpleasant temperament. They are ambush predators that quickly devour smaller fishes, although they are often kept with large cichlids.

Genus *Cichlasoma*

Port Cichlid

Cichlasoma portalagrense, the Port Cichlid, is a true old-timer in fishkeeping, being one of the first South American cichlids kept in aquariums. This very attractive fish is well mannered and easy to keep. It's as close to bulletproof as a fish is likely to be, undemanding as to water chemistry and even diet. Ports are excellent parents; both the male and the female guard and care for the young.

Genus *Geophagus*

Pearl Cichlid

The Pearl Cichlid, *Geophagus brasiliensis,* is a beautiful fish with pearly markings from the eastern coast of South America. Pearl Cichlids are fairly peaceful for large cichlids that reach 8 to 12 inches long. Older males develop an attractive hump on the forehead. These fish require live foods as part of their diet.

Members of the Geophagus *genus are inclined to dig through the substrate* (Geophagus hondae).

Geophagus means "earth-eater," so be prepared to see this fish picking up big mouthfuls of sand and expelling it through its gills. Keep earth-eaters in large tanks decorated with driftwood, rocks and fine substrate.

Genus *Gymnogeophagus*

Balzanii

Gymnogeophagus balzanii, Balzanii, is an 8-inch fish that gives every impression of being huge; the males sport a large cranial hump at sexual maturity. This is a fine-looking golden fish with metallic blue stripes and large elegant fins. Females are smaller and have smaller fins, and don't have the blue striping or the head growth you see in males.

This fish is well worth the large tank and dedicated care required. Because Balzaniis do not tolerate poor water quality, the water must be clean and warm. Balzaniis are aggressive and territorial, and there should be two females for every male. Be prepared to use a tank divider if the fish-play gets rough.

GENUS *Heros*

Salvini

Heros salvini, the Salvini, is a gem from Central America, brilliantly colored with yellow, red, blue and black. Salvini isn't the calmest of fish, having a territorial and aggressive temperament, but it does well in a large tank with a community of like-minded and like-sized cichlids. Male Salvinis reach about 7 inches long; the females grow to about 6 inches. Give them water with a neutral pH or medium hardness level, with temperatures between 72° and 77°F. The tank should have open areas for swimming and a fine-grained, deep substrate. Include live and frozen foods in their diet.

Severum

Heros severus, the Severum, is a popular cichlid from South America. It is also commonly known as the Banded Cichlid. Although the Severum can grow to a respectable 12 inches, it's very attractive, with large red eyes and a rich color. Many hobbyists elect to give it a 50-gallon tank of its own with just a few tough catfish and large dither fish. The Severum is generally a peaceful fish but squabbles with other Severums at breeding time. Severums enjoy green foods, so keeping them in a planted tank can be difficult, although they aren't usually too hard on the tank or its furnishings.

Flag Cichlid

The Flag Cichlid, *Heros festivus,* is one of the shy, generally peaceful cichlids often kept in beautifully planted community tanks. (Your dealer may refer to this fish as Festivum.) Flag Cichlids hail from the Amazon Basin and are usually found in habitats similar to those of angelfish and discus. It's a good fish for a community tank that includes catfish, angelfish, and

large tetras. Just be certain that the tankmates are too large to fit into the Flag Cichlid's mouth.

GENUS *Pterophyllum*

Angelfish

The angelfish, *Pterophyllum scalare,* is very popular with aquarists. Originally, this fish comes from South America, but most of the specimens you see in pet shops have been bred and raised on fish farms. There are many types of angelfish, from the original scalare-type, with a silver body and black stripes, to albinos, marbles, gold and black. You might also find beautiful long-finned angels available. The angelfish is an excellent cichlid for the beginner: It's relatively easy to sustain, doesn't uproot or eat plants, dig, destroy the tank or unduly harass tankmates. Yes, angelfish are still cichlids, so they become somewhat aggressive at spawning time, but not to the point where they're difficult to keep.

AN ANGELFISH WARNING

The angelfish's scientific name, *Pterophyllum scalare,* means "winged leaf; like a flight of stairs." The lovely long fins of this fish explain its name, but beware—those long fins are also a great target for fin-nippers in the tank.

Easy to keep and exceptionally beautiful, angelfish are popular with hobbyists (Pterophyllum scalare).

Although most tank-raised angels are fine in neutral water conditions, they do prefer soft and slightly acidic water, especially for egg hatching. They need a warm tank with temperatures between 78° and 82°F.

Angels accept a wide variety of foods, from flake to small pellets to frozen and live foods. These fish are eager eaters, so if they're fed well and kept in good, clean water, they develop into a nice 4- or 5-inch fish with long, trailing fins and good color.

Genus *Symphysodon*

Discus

Symphysodon discus, the discus, is the regent of the fish world. It's well-known for its outstanding appearance and challenging keeping requirements. Found in the black waters of Amazonia, discus need very clean, soft and acidic (pH from 5.0 to 6.5) water, as well as high temperatures of 82° to 86°F. The tank should have a fine sand substrate with driftwood and plenty of plants. Breeders often keep discus in bare tanks with only a sponge filter because decorations make it more difficult to keep the tank sufficiently clean.

Discus are fond of beef heart, bloodworms, brine shrimp and whiteworms, but it's best to include prepared foods in their diet, too. They are essentially bottom feeders that blow into the substrate in the hope of finding little tidbits. They are leisurely diners, so don't be too hasty to remove leftover food. Give them at least an hour to consume each meal.

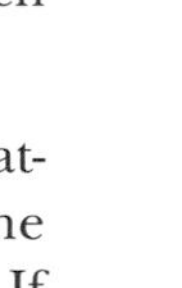

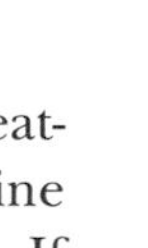

Discus enjoy a large, deep tank (Symphysodon discus).

You may find that new acquisitions are slow to start eating. If they have been traumatized by travel, live brine shrimp or frozen bloodworms usually tempt them. If they do not soon "take the bait," the fish could be ill.

Discus are not generally considered a good fish for beginners, but those who are willing to discover how to keep them and invest the time and effort to care for them properly can be very successful. Even though discus are a bit more work than most aquarium fish, it's rewarding to see them grow, pair up and perhaps spawn in the aquarium.

Discus are exceptional in the care and feeding of their young. Although cichlids are almost always good parents, discus take this trait one step further. Both the male and the female provide food for the young in the form of "discus milk" that the fry eat from the sides of their bodies.

Unfortunately, discus are sensitive to parasites and often must be treated for diseases before they can thrive in the aquarium. There's no room for compromise or neglect when you're keeping discus. They must have the proper care and water conditions.

The spots on the Uaru disappear as it ages.

Genus *Uaru*

Uaru

Uaru amphiacanthoides, the Uaru (also known as the Triangle Cichlid or Waroo), is another popular cichlid from South America. Uarus are not often available, and they aren't easy to keep, but they are well worth the effort once you have mastered the formula for keeping South American cichlids; water should be peaty, soft, acidic and warm.

Uarus are peaceful schooling fish, timid and shy, even though they can grow to 12 inches long. They are primarily herbivores, so they require plenty of fresh vegetable foods in addition to flakes and frozen foods to thrive. Follow the same guidelines for keeping discus, but include more greens in the diet.

Aquariums for North and Central American Cichlids

The North and Central American fish are particularly easy to keep with respect to water chemistry, usually favoring water on the hard and alkaline side with pH levels between 7.0 and 8.0. Most Central American cichlids, however, are quite comfortable in neutral water or even slightly acidic conditions. The temperature should be kept in the mid- to high-70s, but some of the more northern species accept lower temperatures periodically.

Because both appetite and aggressiveness are related to water temperature, one trick used by aquarists is to keep the larger, more belligerent species at the low end of their recommended temperature range.

These fishes can be kept in community tanks as long as size, behavior, diet and water requirements are known and taken into consideration. As with any cichlid, their best chance for success is when youngsters of the differing species are reared together as a "family." A hierarchy will emerge, but it's less traumatic than if you try to introduce the same kind of fish as adults.

Most of the common aquarium species are small to medium in size—up to 6 inches long—which means you can usually keep them in tanks of about 30 gallons. For fish longer than 6 inches, increase the tank size to 40 to 100 gallons.

North and Central American cichlids are omnivorous, so offer them both pellets and fresh greens, such as Romaine lettuce, parsley, zucchini and spinach. Be careful to avoid overfeeding. Even though these fishes have hearty appetites, they waste a lot of food and place a serious strain on your filtration system.

North American and Central American Species

Genus *Amphilophus*

Emerald Cichlid

Amphilophus robertsoni, the Emerald Cichlid, is one stunning fish, boasting a spangled turquoise body shot with red around the fins. At 7 inches long, it's not overly large, but it can be a bit nasty, nonetheless.

Emerald cichlids like to sift through the gravel for food, so give them a medium- or fine-grained smooth substrate.

Midas Cichlid

The Midas Cichlid, *Amphilophus citrinellum,* is a native of Nicaragua and Costa Rica. Keep this fish in alkaline water with a pH of 7 to 8.5. The Midas Cichlid is a real show fish, with an orange, white and yellow spangled body and an elaborate hump on the male's forehead. You can expect to see a good deal of aggression with this fish, but with a big tank, you will have a real conversation piece.

To keep the peace, consider keeping Convict Cichlids in a species tank.

Genus *Archocentrus*

Convict Cichlid

Archocentrus nigrofasciatus, the Convict Cichlid, is a mean little fish that grows up to 6 inches long. However, the Convict is incredibly easy to keep and breed. This Central American fish is a real "bread and butter" cichlid, despite its tendency to eat plants, dig destructively and rip the fins of its tankmates. The advantages of this fish are its attractive blue-gray body with black stripes, its great appetite, and the strong pair bond it forms, with both parents caring for the young. Give the Convict a large tank with caves and rocks.

Jack Dempsey

Named for a heavyweight champion of the 1920s, the Jack Dempsey is a pugnacious cichlid.

Archocentrus octofasciatum, more commonly known as the Jack Dempsey, often lands in the mixed cichlid community. It's a good-looking 8-inch fish with bright blue iridescence, a hefty body and an attitude. The problem is that Jack Dempseys become very territorial as they mature. If you want to keep them in a community tank, start out with all young like-sized tankmates and let them grow up together with plenty of hiding places. The Jack Dempsey isn't a *bad* fish; it just needs to protect its space, and does so with all the energy of its prizefighter namesake. Give this fish lots of room and meaty foods, and it will grow into a real beauty. For the Jack Dempsey, the pH should be between 6.5 and 7.0 and the temperature around 77°F.

Blue-Eyed Cichlid

Archocentrus spilurus, the Blue-Eyed Cichlid, is a well-established aquarium resident that grows from 4 to 5 inches long (females are slightly larger). Mature males have distinctly pointed dorsal and anal fins, and adult females occasionally develop a hump on the forehead.

These peaceful fish tolerate plants well, but, like nearly every other cichlid, they can get rowdy at spawning time.

Give this fish plenty of caves, a gravelly substrate and floating plants for security.

Genus *Herichthys*

Texas Cichlid

Herichthys cyanoguttatus, the beautiful, pearly patterned Texas Cichlid, is found in the rivers and lakes of Texas and northern Mexico. Its size ranges from 5 to 12 inches. The Texas Cichlid requires very clean water with frequent partial changes. The water temperature can be kept at about 68° to 75°F, not quite as warm as that for most of the other cichlids. The water can be neutral to slightly acidic.

This bad-tempered fish should be kept only with fish that can defend themselves well. Use a fine substrate and barriers of rock. Live and frozen foods are much appreciated, but Texas Cichlids accept large pellets, too.

The Managuense is not particular and will harass other species as well as other Managuense.

Genus *Nandopsis*

Nandopsis managuense

Nandopsis managuense, the Managuense, is an 11-inch monster fish. In fishkeeping circles, the name *Managuense* is synonymous with "beastly behavior." This fish is a biter, a digger, a plant destroyer and a real tank-buster. Managuense are difficult to keep because of their behavior but are easy as far as water chemistry is concerned, preferring medium values in pH and hardness. The temperature should be in the low 70s. Feed Managuense lots of live foods, such as fish, insects and earthworms, along with pellets and frozen foods.

Genus *Thorichthys*

Firemouth

Thorichthys meeki, the Firemouth, is a sharp-looking fish from Central America. The body is in shades of blue, and its iridescence is set off by brilliant red on the belly and gills. The Fire-mouth is so named because when it's threatened, it displays its bright red gill covers and throat sac, giving the appearance of a much larger and more aggressive fish. Unless it believes itself under attack, the Firemouth is not exceptionally aggressive. It's territorial and defensive when spawning, but otherwise makes a good community tank fish.

Omnivorous Firemouths happily consume live, frozen and flake foods.

Firemouths do dig a bit but don't go out of their way to destroy plants, as a rule. Give them neutral water conditions, some rocks and driftwood territories and a fine-grained substrate. Omnivores, Firemouths will eat live, frozen, or flake food.

part four

Beyond the Basics

chapter 11

Resources for the Aquarist

Clubs

The American Cichlid Association (ACA)

The American Cichlid Association is the premiere cichlid club in the United States, with an annual convention that draws cichlid lovers from all over the world. The official monthly journal of the ACA, *The Buntbarsche Bulletin,* is included with membership.

American Cichlid Association
Membership Chairman
P.O. Box 5351
Naperville, IL 60567-5351

Local Cichlid Club

Southern California Cichlid Association
4195 Chino Hills Parkway
Chino Hills, CA 91709

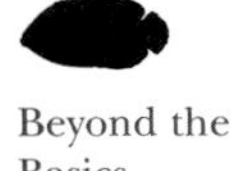

Cichlid Clubs Around the World

Queensland Cichlid Group
P.O. Box 360
Wooloongabba, Queensland 4102
Australia

Perth Cichlid Society Incorporated
P.O. Box 323
Gosnells, WA 6990
Australia

Deutsche Cichliden Geselischaft
Strabe 1-9/1/3/12
A-1220 Wien
Austria

Belgische Cichliden Vereninging
Kievitlaan 23
B-2288 Ransl
Belgium

Dansk Cichlide Selskab
Tølløsevej 76
DK-2700 Brøshøj
Denmark

British Cichlid Association
248 Longridge
Knutsford Cheshire, WA 18 8PH
England

Association France Cichlids
15 Rue des Hirondelles
F-87350, Dauendorf
France

Aquaristischer Arbeitskreis Leinetal
Interessegemeinshaft Cichliden
Ludwig-Prandtl-Strabe 56
D-37077 Gottingen
Germany

CichlidenKlub Essen
Lohstrabe 39
D-45359 Essen
Germany